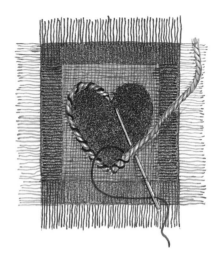

appliqué

The COUNTRY LIVING Needlework Collection

appliqué

projects · techniques · motifs

Lucinda Ganderton

Photography by Pia Tryde

Quadrille

pages 1 and 5: Herb Bags (see page 82)
page 2: Floral Tablecloth (see page 74)
page 3: Broderie Perse Throw (see page 66)

Illustrations • Kate Simunek
Pattern & motif drawings • Keith Jackson

First published in 1996 by
Quadrille Publishing Limited
9 Irving Street, London WC2H 7AT

Published in association with the National Magazine Company Limited
Country Living is a trademark of the National Magazine Company Limited

Art Director • Mary Evans
Managing Editor • Jane O'Shea
Art Editor • Vanessa Courtier
Project Editor • Patsy North
Copy Editor • Sarah Widdicombe
Editorial Assistant • Katherine Seely

British Library Cataloguing-in-Publication Data
A catalogue record for this book is available
from the British Library.

ISBN 1 899988 75 0

Printed in Spain

contents

Introduction

Appliqué can be defined simply as the process of stitching a small piece of cloth on to a contrasting larger one. At a time when woven fabrics were scarce, the unworn parts of a garment would be salvaged and used to repair clothing or furnishings. It was a logical progression for the applied fabric to be cut out in interesting shapes to form a new design, and then stitched down in a decorative manner. From its early utilitarian origins – examples have been found even in ancient Egyptian tombs – the basic process of patching has become a highly versatile needlecraft.

There is a vast international heritage of appliqué, providing an exciting source of inspiration upon which we can build today. Many different cultures have evolved their own ways of working, often utilizing locally available materials in addition to woven fabrics. Native Americans collected dried leaves, beetle wings and porcupine quills to decorate leather shapes; the Inuits of Alaska used fish skin and feathers; and the bold, bright processional canopies made in India were adorned with dazzling fragments of *shisha* mirror to reflect the sunlight. Tibetan costume and temple hangings, along with *mola cloths* from San Blas in Central America, feature intricate 'reverse appliqué', which involves cutting into layers of fabric rather than adding to them.

American appliqué, which is inextricably linked with patchwork and quilting, is still the best-known and most widely practised method. Applied motifs are often incorporated with patchwork to bring a softer, more flowing element to the designs. Stylized designs of flowers, foliage, cornucopias and shells, with evocative names such as Meadow Lily, Princess Feather, Seek No Further and Horn of Plenty, became a showcase for needlework skills.

There is a certain satisfaction and sense of continuity in recreating an old pattern, and interest in textile history is widespread. However, needleworkers have always been innovative. This book is intended both as a guide to traditional hand appliqué and as an introduction to newer methods. The projects range from those suitable for a complete beginner to more complex designs for the experienced worker. Drawing on a wealth of tradition, they incorporate a wide range of imagery, fabrics, textures and embroidery stitches, to convey an overall impression that is unmistakably contemporary.

Getting started

Traditional appliqué techniques have been used by successive generations of needleworkers and quiltmakers worldwide to create a vast array of formal and informal, naturalistic and geometric designs. The traditional turned-edge method has a bold and direct quality which produces sharply defined shapes, and it can be used to produce an almost infinite range of patterns, from simple squares to intricate floral or pictorial motifs.

Only the most basic of sewing skills are required to fix one piece of cloth on to another, but today there are new ways of doing this. Comparatively recent developments in bonding fabrics, and the imaginative use of the domestic sewing machine, have both speeded up the process and opened up different ways of working. This chapter introduces the simple tools and equipment needed, and then explores the long-established techniques of folded-edge and pattern-cut appliqué, along with contemporary methods of machine appliqué.

materials & equipment

Like its allied needlecrafts of patchwork and quilting, hand appliqué does not require any expensive or specialized tools. All you need to get started is a basic sewing kit of needles and pins, scissors, a tape measure and a selection of threads. You will be investing a great deal of time and care in your work, so it is always worth selecting the best-quality tools and materials in order to achieve a lasting and professional result.

Sewing machines are becoming increasingly sophisticated and many are now electronically controlled. However, a well-maintained ordinary swing-needle model is all that is required for most machine-appliqué projects.

Sewing tools

All your needlework equipment should be stored safely in one place. This can range from a purpose-made workbox with separate compartments for each item, to a simple wicker basket lined with cotton fabric. A traditional housewife, or sewing roll, is still a useful way of keeping essential small items to hand, and instructions for making a felt appliqué version are given on pages 50–2.

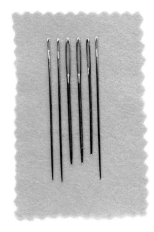

Needles
Needles for hand sewing are available in a range of sizes, each with its own particular purpose. The thickness of the needle should always be matched to the weight of fabric with which you are working. It is a good idea to buy a packet of needles in mixed sizes to begin with, and transfer them to a needlecase for safekeeping. The shiny plated finish wears off with use, and you should discard any tarnished or blunted needles.
• Medium-length 'sharps' are used for general hand sewing on most types of fabric, and are useful for tacking and stitching down appliqué shapes.
• The shorter 'betweens' (quilting needles) are good for working slip stitch, as their small size helps to keep the stitches regular and neat.

• Crewel needles are used primarily for embroidery. They have an extra-long eye through which thicker threads can pass without becoming snagged.

Pins
Dressmaker's pins are essential for holding pieces of fabric together before tacking and for keeping motifs in place before they are sewn down. A well-stuffed pincushion is the best way of keeping your pins safely and conveniently to hand.
• Special brass lacemaking pins are slightly longer and finer than standard pins, and are less likely to leave marks in the fabric.
• Glass-headed pins are helpful when working on larger areas or on thicker fabrics, as they are easily visible.

Thimble

Thimbles are a practical way to protect your fingers when sewing for a long stretch of time. They are available in wood, metal or plastic, and should fit snugly but not too tightly.

Scissors

Scissors are important tools and the blades should always be sharp. It is useful to have four different pairs, each kept for its particular use:

• Medium-sized sewing scissors, which are easier to handle than large dressmaking shears, for cutting out background and appliqué fabrics.
• Small embroidery scissors with narrow, sharply pointed blades, for trimming and notching seam allowances and for clipping off threads.
• Paper scissors, for cutting out templates and tacking papers.
• Pinking shears, to give a decorative edge to a cut-out shape.

Drawing and transferring equipment

You will need a small supply of basic art materials for making templates and planning out appliqué designs. In addition, you will need some specialized dressmaker's equipment for transferring your designs on to fabric, all of which is readily available at haberdashery and craft shops.

Drawing equipment

A basic selection of drawing materials should include the following items:
• Tracing paper, thin card and thick paper.
• Clear plastic ruler and set square.
• Pencils and eraser.
• Pair of compasses, for drawing accurate curves and circles.
• Long ruler, for measuring and marking on to fabric.

Transferring designs

Designs can be transferred on to fabric in a number of ways.
• Dressmaker's carbon paper can be used to trace a template or an entire design directly on to fabric and is available in both light and dark colours.
• Dressmaker's pens produce an ink line which will fade completely in time, or which is water soluble. This makes them ideal for marking round templates or for drawing freehand on to fabric.
• Transfer pencils and pens can be used to trace or draw an accurate outline on to thin paper. This is then transferred on to the fabric by dry ironing from the back or simply by applying pressure, depending on the type of marker used.
• Chalk marking pencils or tailor's chalk are more traditional ways of marking shapes, and make a line that can be brushed away easily.

Fabrics and trimmings

It is, of course, possible to sew any two types of fabric together, but for the most durable results you should choose materials of similar weights, such as finely woven natural cottons, shirting and dress prints. Avoid thicker fabrics or those which stretch or fray easily. Printed textiles, translucent fabrics and fancy trimmings can also be effective for appliqué; try experimenting with unusual combinations, as seemingly unrelated fabrics can often work together to provide an unexpectedly dramatic result.

• Background fabrics for appliqué should always have a firm, close weave and be strong enough to support a lot of stitching, but they can be reinforced with iron-on interfacing if necessary. If an item is going to receive a lot of wear or will need to be laundered, all the fabrics should be washed and pressed before cutting out to ensure that they will not shrink and are colourfast.

• It is not always necessary to buy expensive fabrics for appliqué. Collect together scraps, offcuts and remnants – the random selection of the ragbag can be inspiring in its mixture of textures and shapes. Lace, organzas and ribbons, for example, can be combined with printed furnishing fabrics, velvets or woven brocades for an extravagant effect.

• If you cannot find exactly the right fabric for an appliqué project, it is not difficult to add colour and pattern to a length of plain white cotton fabric to create your own personal design, and the results can be very satisfying. There are many special fabric paints available in liquid and tube form, and these can be used to paint areas of plain colour, to print simple designs from basic blocks, or to draw striped or geometric designs from which motifs can be cut. The colourful motifs on the Kitchen curtains on page 46 have been created from fabric painted in this way.

• Individual motifs can be cut out from strongly patterned fabrics such as bold floral prints or *toiles de Jouy* and rearranged on a plain background to make a fresh design. The motifs can then be embellished with hand or machine embroidery for further decoration.This technique is known as *broderie perse* (see Broderie perse throw on page 66).

Threads Ordinary sewing thread is used for tacking and for stitching motifs on to a background, either by hand or by machine. The more ornamental embroidery cottons, silks and yarns, which come in various weights and textures, can be used to embellish your appliqué designs.

Sewing threads

These are available in various thicknesses, different-sized reels and many colours. Take time to match the thread to the fabric as closely as possible; choose the deeper shade when sewing dark fabrics on to a light background and vice versa. Use a contrasting thread when tacking, so that the stitches can be unpicked easily.

• All-purpose polyester thread is versatile enough for most general use. To prevent fraying when sewing appliqué shapes by hand, it can be strengthened by running a length over a block of beeswax.

• Specially produced quilting thread is made from a mixture of cotton and polyester and has a glacé finish. It is particularly strong, which makes it ideal for hand stitching heavier fabrics.

• Cotton or polyester-mix threads are designed for ordinary machine use and dressmaking. Machine embroidery threads will give a lustrous finish to satin stitch, but for a very special effect try using finely spun silk or metallic threads.

Embroidery threads

Select embroidery threads to contrast or co-ordinate with a design – there is a vast spectrum of colours from which to choose. Threads as diverse as silk buttonhole twist, crewel wool and soft embroidery cotton will all give a different decorative effect, but the weight of the yarn should always be compatible with the fabrics you are using.

• Stranded cotton is the most popular and versatile embroidery thread. Its six loosely spun threads can be used together for a chunky look, or separated out – two or three strands are commonly used for finer stitching.

• Pearl cotton (*coton perlé*) consists of a single, tightly spun thread. It comes in three thicknesses and gives an attractive, shiny finish to the stitches.

• Soft embroidery cotton is a thick thread with a matt finish, ideal for bold, decorative stitching.

• Crewel wool is a fine, matt yarn that can be used very effectively for decorating woollen fabrics and felt.

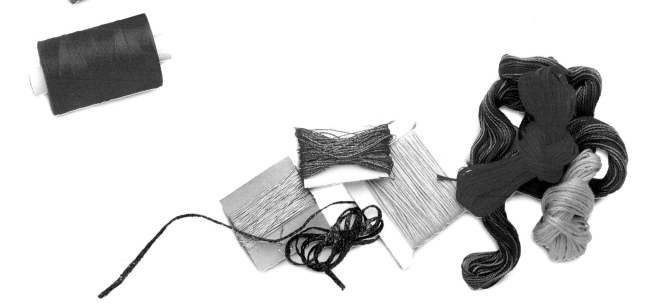

hand appliqué

Turned-edge appliqué could not be more straightforward and the technique is quick to master. The design is simply drawn on to a piece of cloth, cut out, neatened and sewn on to a background. Closely woven fabrics such as cotton lawn are the best choice to start with, as they do not fray quickly and are easy to handle. Get the feel of how to appliqué by starting off with straight-edged shapes; then, with practice, elaborate curves and geometric patterns can be achieved.

Making the templates

Appliqué patterns are usually drawn to their exact size without any additional seam allowance, so that they can be traced and transferred accurately on to the fabric. The seam allowance is then added on. The patterns for most of the designs in this book are provided at a reduced scale, and will have to be enlarged to the size required before they are traced. This is easily done using a photocopier – the instructions for the project will specify the enlargement required.

For a single appliqué motif which will be used just once, a paper shape can be cut out directly from the photocopy or the tracing. If the motif is to be repeated several times in a design, the outline should be transferred on to thin card to make a more lasting template. When working with complex, multi-layered designs, trace off all the individual elements. Make a separate template for each shape and label them carefully to avoid confusion later.

Transferring the designs

fig 1

1 Place the template on the right side of the fabric and line it up along the grain. It is important to match the grain of the cut-out shape to that of the background fabric whenever possible, especially when cutting out larger shapes. This prevents the two finished layers pulling in different directions and puckering.
2 Secure a paper template by pinning through the centre rather than around the outside edge, to prevent the fabric becoming distorted. Hold a card template in place with one hand. Mark around the template with a sharp chalk marking pencil or dressmaker's fading pen, keeping the line close to the edge of the template.
3 Mark in the seam allowance by drawing a second outline 6mm (¼in) outside the first (fig 1). Remove the template and cut out the motif along the outside line. If you are using a non-woven fabric, such as felt or suede, there is no need to add any extra allowance, while one that frays easily will need a wider turning.

Preparing the shapes

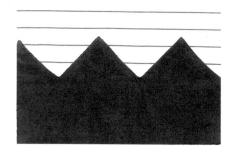

Once the appliqué pieces have been cut out, the raw edges will need to be neatened by turning them to the wrong side, tacking them down and pressing lightly. The tacking stitches are unpicked once the piece has been sewn down on its background; make sure all knots in the tacking thread lie on top of the fabric so that they can easily be removed. For straight-sided shapes, the seam allowance can simply be folded under without further preparation; curves and angles on a shape are a bit more complicated to deal with as the seam allowance will pucker up or pull if it is not prepared properly before being turned under.

Peaks and valleys

Sharp corners and inside angles are often found on floral or geometric shapes. To get a precise outline, the surplus fabric around them has to be either clipped back or opened up, so that the shape will lie flat.

fig 2

Mitring peaks

1 Trim off the outside point, then cut back the extra fabric for a short distance on either side to within 3mm (⅛in) of the outline (fig 2).

2 Fold the point over to the wrong side as far as the marked line, then turn back the seam allowance on the two adjacent sides and tack in place (fig 3). Secure the peak with a few overstitches when you are sewing it on to the background fabric (see page 17).

Turning valleys

1 For an inside corner, or 'valley', clip the seam allowance vertically to the inside point of the angle, right up to the marked line (fig 4).

2 Turn back the seam allowance on either side of the cut and tack it down (fig 5). To prevent the angle from fraying, reinforce it with a few overstitches when you are sewing it on to the background fabric (see page 17).

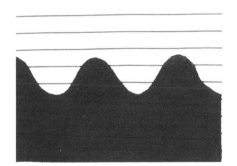

fig 3

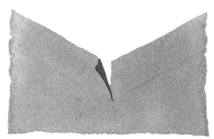

fig 4

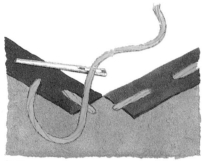

fig 5

Curves

The seam allowance along shallow curves can simply be gently gathered under, but where the curve is tight the allowance will need to be snipped before being turned, using small, sharp scissors. The tighter the curve, the closer together the cuts should be.

1 Cut into inside (concave) curved edges at right angles, up to 3mm (⅛in) from the marked outline. For outside (convex) curves, remove the excess fabric by

cutting out evenly spaced small notches to 3mm (⅛in) from the outline (fig 6).

2 Turn the seam allowance to the wrong side and tack in place (fig 7).

fig 6

fig 7

Tacking over papers

fig 1

fig 2

Multi-petalled flowers and circles can be fiddly to sew, and when working on a small scale it is not always easy to clip and stitch the seam allowances neatly. An effective method of dealing with this problem is to turn the raw edges of the fabric motifs over cut-out paper or card shapes which exactly match the templates.

Circles

1 Cut out a disc of thin card to the exact size required. From fabric, cut out a circle 12mm (½ in) larger in diameter than the disc and run a line of closely spaced gathering stitches around the edge. Place the cardboard centrally on the wrong side of the fabric.

2 Draw up the thread so that the fabric encloses the disc, and arrange the gathers so that they lie evenly and give a smooth outline (fig 1). Press from the right side, then remove the disc carefully, without distorting the fabric circle.

Flowers

1 First draw around the flower template on to thick paper and cut out the motif. Then cut out the fabric shape as usual, leaving a 6mm (¼ in) seam allowance all round, and pin the paper shape centrally to the wrong side.

2 Turn back the seam allowance, clipping where necessary, and tack it in place through the paper, making sure there are no creases (fig 2). Press the shape from the right side using a pressing cloth, then remove the tacking thread and take out the paper.

Making bias strips

Many appliqué designs feature narrow bands or stripes, such as flower stalks. When these are straight, the fabric is cut along the grain, but curved lines should be cut on the bias, at 45° to the grain. This makes a flexible strip that will lie flat without puckering. Strips that are less than 6mm (¼ in) wide are difficult to handle as the edges tend to fray, so 'rouleau' strips are often used for these.

Turned-edge strips

1 Cut out a paper template that measures 12mm (½ in) wider than the finished strip. Pin this diagonally across the fabric and cut out (fig 3).

2 Press under 6mm (¼ in) seam allowances along either side of the strip. Tack these down and press lightly, then sew in place.

Rouleau strips

1 Cut out a strip of fabric to twice the required width, plus 12mm (½ in). With right sides together, fold the strip in half lengthways and stitch by hand or machine 6mm (¼ in) from the outside edge. Trim back the seam allowance to 3mm (⅛ in) (fig 4).

2 Turn the rouleau through by threading a large tapestry needle with a length of cotton or wool and securing the end firmly to one open end of the strip. Pass the needle right through the tube of fabric so that the rouleau is turned right side out (fig 5). Press so that the seam lies at the centre back of the strip.

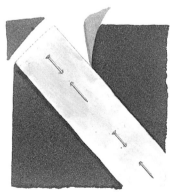

fig 3

fig 4

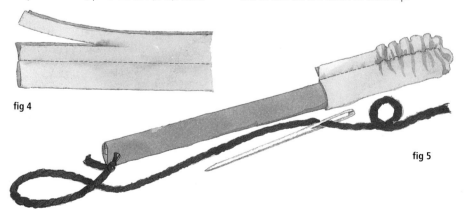

fig 5

Assembling the design

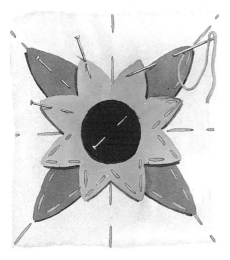

fig 6

Most straightforward shapes can simply be positioned on the background fabric by eye, referring back to the original pattern, but geometric or symmetrical designs need to be planned so that the pieces are positioned accurately and overlapping shapes are stitched down in the correct order. For a complex design, dressmaker's carbon paper or a transfer pencil can be used to trace the entire outline on to the background as a guide for placing the pieces.

Symmetrical designs

Work these logically, so that the bottom layers of a multi-layered design are pinned down first, then the smaller and more detailed pieces are placed on top.
1 Fold the background fabric into quarters horizontally, vertically and diagonally, and press lightly. Mark the creases with contrasting tacking stitches. Fold the paper design tracing in the same way, so that the two sets of guidelines can be matched.
2 Pin, then tack down the individual shapes (fig 6), using a ruler as a guide if necessary. Insert the pins at right angles to the edge if possible, not parallel, so that the pieces lie flat, and smooth out any wrinkles or puckers as you work.

Tension

To ensure a really smooth finish, small areas of appliqué can be stitched in an embroidery hoop and larger pieces mounted in a square frame. This maintains an even tension across the background and prevents the shapes from distorting. However, it is not essential: if you work on a flat surface and pin and tack each shape carefully, there is no real need to use a frame.

Stitching the motifs

fig 7

fig 8

fig 9

Appliqué shapes can be sewn down in several ways, depending on the finished effect you want. Running stitch is the most basic way of joining any two pieces of fabric and, along with overstitch, can be used for non-fraying fabrics. Slip stitch is the traditional method of securing folded-edge appliqué. All three methods can be embellished further with embroidery stitches (see pages 39–41 in the Decorative Stitching chapter).

Running stitch is used when the line of stitching is intended to show, and can be worked in a contrasting colour if required. The length of the individual stitches can be varied according to the scale of the work, but they must all be equal and evenly spaced (fig 7).
Slip stitch gives an almost invisible join. Make small, neat stitches, no more than 6mm (¼in) apart, being careful not to pull the thread too tightly. Bring the needle up just inside the motif, then back over the folded edge and through the background fabric (fig 8).
Overstitch is often used for shapes without a seam allowance. The thread overlaps the edge of the motif and prevents it fraying (fig 9). Several overstitches, worked at right angles, are used to reinforce the turning of a valley or secure the tip of a peak (see page 15).

Finishing off

Careful pressing, preferably with a steam iron, will give a crisp, professional finish to your work. When all the shapes have been sewn in place, remove all the tacking threads. Press the finished piece from the wrong side on to a padded surface, such as a clean folded tea towel, using a pressing cloth so that the seam allowances do not show through.

denim flags

This project uses the simplest methods of hand sewing to dramatic effect, and incorporates the thrift element that lay behind much of the earliest appliqué. The faded indigo tones of old, well-washed denim are combined with plain stripes and small-scale prints, some of which were salvaged from an irreparably damaged antique quilt.

The simple shapes, highlighted with contrast stitching, are reminiscent of both national flags and nautical signals. Rather than being neatened, the edges of the flags have been left raw to become a decorative feature in themselves, while pinking shears have been used to give a zigzag finish to the applied shapes.

You will need

Old denim jeans
Old or new striped and printed cotton fabric scraps in red, white and blue
Contrasting stranded cottons
Crewel needle
Pinking shears

To make up

1 Press the jeans, then check over the lower part of the legs to find areas that show interesting signs of wear. Using a ruler and set square, mark out 3 rectangles on the denim, each 20 x 17cm (8 x 6¾in). Ensure that each incorporates part of the leg seam, 3.5cm (1½in) from one short edge. Cut out the rectangles following the grain of the fabric, then pull out a few threads along each side to make a small fringe.

2 Cut out 3 rectangles, each 7 x 11cm (3 x 4½in), from different striped fabrics, with the stripes running parallel to the long sides. Cut carefully along the grain of the fabric. Again, pull out a few threads along each side to make a small frayed edge.

3 Tack the striped rectangles to the denim ones so that one short edge lies centrally along the seam. Thread a crewel needle with 2 strands of contrasting stranded cotton and stitch down the rectangles using a small, regular running stitch, about 6mm (¼in) from the frayed edge of the striped fabric. The stitches and spaces in between them should not be more than 3mm (⅛in) long.

4 Choose 4 contrasting print fabrics for the appliqué shapes. Using pinking shears, cut out rectangles 5 x 3.5cm (2 x 1½in), or 4cm (1⅝in) squares. Tack, then stitch them in place with running stitch, again using a contrasting stranded cotton (fig 1). Press the finished piece from the wrong side.

fig 1

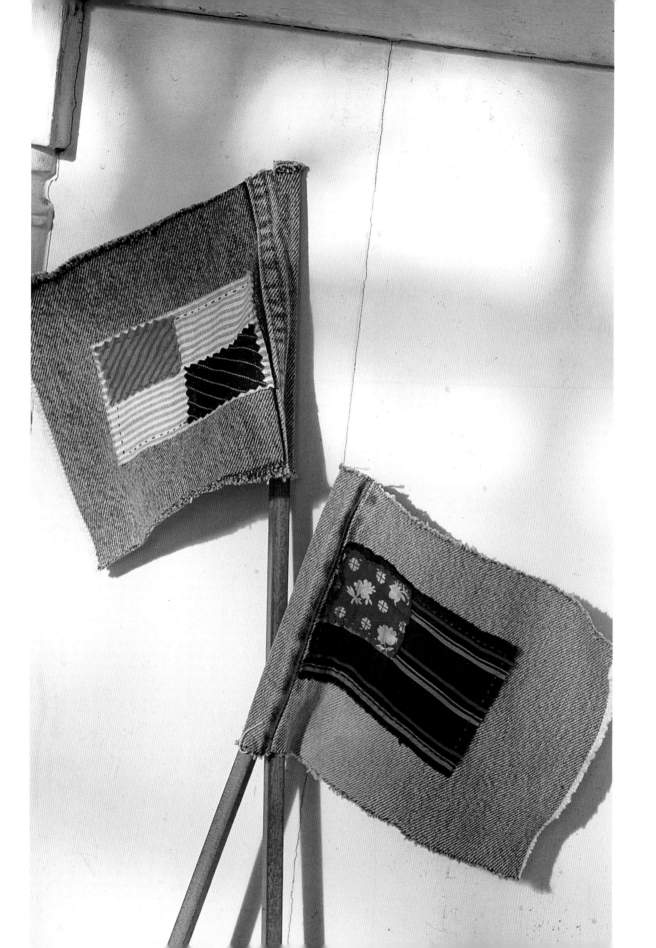

baltimore bride cushion

This American folk-art style cushion is adapted from a single block of a lavish wedding quilt made in Baltimore in the mid-nineteenth century. The rose design was a favourite appliqué pattern, and there are many realistic and stylized variations to be found. This symmetrical version has a large central flower which is balanced by matching buds and smaller blue flowers. Its fresh, contemporary look is achieved by using bold primary colours on a crisp cotton pinstripe background. The cushion is edged with matching piping, but the finishing touch is at the back, where brightly covered buttons are held in place with rouleau buttonhole loops. The ambitious quilter could repeat the motif to make a bed cover. Further traditional floral patterns are provided on pages 98–99.

You will need

For a cushion 50cm (20in) square:
1.4m (1⅝yd) blue-and-white pinstripe shirting, 150cm (60in) wide
54cm (21in) square medium-weight iron-on interfacing
Plain cotton lawn or sheeting:
    25 x 50cm (10 x 19½in) red
    25 x 30cm (10 x 12in) blue and green
    10 x 30cm (4 x 12in) yellow
Sewing threads in red, green, blue, yellow and white
2.1m (84in) medium piping cord
8 self-cover buttons, 2.5cm (1in) diameter
Cushion pad, 50cm (20in) square

To prepare the appliqué

1 Enlarge the pattern on page 22 to 150% on a photocopier. Make the templates by tracing the 8 separate design elements – the large flower and 2 parts of its centre, the small flower with its centre, the leaf, the stem and the bud – on to thin card. Draw carefully around these on to thick paper to make the tacking papers: 1 large flower with centre, 4 small flowers with centres, 16 leaves, 8 stems and 4 buds.
2 Cut out the appliqué shapes from cotton fabric, using the card templates and adding 6mm (¼in) all round for the seam allowances.
3 Tack the flowers, leaves and buds over their respective papers, clipping the seam allowances as necessary. Tack the stems to their paper strips, but turn under the long edges only. Press all the pieces, unpick the tacking and remove the papers carefully.

To assemble the design

1 Cut out a 54cm (21in) square of pinstripe shirting for the cushion front and reinforce it with iron-on interfacing. Tack horizontal, vertical and diagonal guidelines across the square in a contrasting colour (see page 17).
2 Referring to fig 1, which illustrates the correct order of assembly, centre and pin down the large red flower. Then pin down the stems along the guidelines, tucking the lower ends under the edges of the petals.

3 Pin down the leaves, then the buds and the small blue corner flowers. Finally, pin down the flower centres.
4 When all the pieces have been positioned correctly, tack them down. Start from the centre and work out to each corner in turn, removing the pins as you go along.
5 Hand sew the appliqué with slip stitch, using different coloured threads to match each shape. Remove all the tacking threads and press lightly from the wrong side.

To make the cushion back
1 Cut 2 rectangles of shirting, 30 x 54cm (12 x 21in) and 36 x 54cm (14 x 21in), with the stripes running parallel to the longer sides, to make the 2 sides of the cushion back. Neaten one long edge of the wider piece with a narrow double hem.
2 Following the instructions on page 16, make buttonhole loops from 8 narrow rouleau strips of shirting, each 8cm (3¼in) long, and attach these to one long edge of the narrower cushion back

Just over a quarter of the design is shown here. Enlarge it to 150% on a photocopier and trace the separate design elements on to thin card. Add a 6mm (1/4 in) seam allowance when cutting out the fabric.

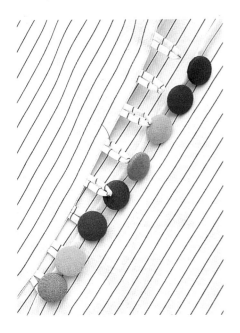

piece. Fold the fabric in half widthways and mark the centre. Pin and tack 4 loops either side of this point so that the ends are level with the edge of the fabric. Leave gaps of 2cm (¾in) between the loops.

3 Cut out a strip of shirting 10 x 54cm (4 x 21in) to make the facing for the buttonhole loops. Neaten one long edge, then pin the facing in place over the buttonhole loops with right sides and cut edges together. Tack, then stitch in place, leaving a seam allowance of 12mm (½in), so that the loops are caught in the seam (fig 2). Turn the facing to the wrong side and press.

To make up

1 From the remaining shirting, cut out bias strips 4cm (1½in) wide, joining them diagonally until they measure 2.1m (84in) long. Cover the piping cord with the bias strips and pin the piping to the cushion front, starting at the bottom edge and matching cut edges.

2 Assemble the 3 pieces of the cushion cover with right sides together. Making sure that all the stripes run from top to bottom, pin the side of the cushion back with the buttonhole loops along one edge, so that the loops point towards the centre. Pin the second side along the opposite edge with the hem facing inwards (fig 3).

3 Using the zip foot, stitch around all 4 sides as close to the piping as possible, leaving a seam allowance of 12mm (½in). Clip the corners and turn the cover right side out. Press lightly.

4 Cover the buttons with plain cotton fabric, following the manufacturer's instructions. Make 2 in each colour and sew them firmly in place on the back of the cushion, so that they line up with the buttonhole loops. Insert the cushion pad and fasten the buttons.

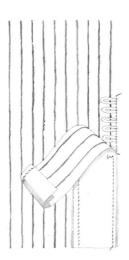

fig 2

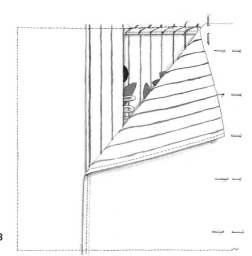

fig 3

machine appliqué

Provided you are familiar with the controls, using your machine to stitch cut-out shapes in place should not prove to be any more complicated than any other sewing or dressmaking technique. Machine stitching gives a distinctive, clear outline to appliqué motifs. It is also quick to do and produces a hardwearing yet decorative finish, which is particularly suitable for embellishing garments, quilts, cushions and any other soft furnishings which will receive a lot of wear or need to be laundered.

Applying the motifs

Motifs for machine appliqué are cut out to their finished size without any additional seam allowance, making the technique ideal for non-woven fabrics such as felt, which can be attached with a straight stitch.

There can be difficulties when working with fabrics that fray. These are usually sewn down with zigzag or satin stitch, and the dense stitching may pull the appliqué out of shape if it is not tacked securely to the background. Alternatively, products to prevent fraying are available from most haberdashers and craft shops. These are painted on to the back of the fabric and allowed to dry thoroughly before cutting out.

Bonding web

Joining the appliqué to the background fabric with bonding web solves the problem of the motifs becoming distorted when machine stitched. The bonding consists of a heat-sensitive adhesive web attached to a paper backing, on to which the motifs are traced. This means that the shapes will not only be accurate, but will also be firmly fixed to the background across their entire surface so that they neither pucker nor fray as the fabric is stitched.

Bonding web is best used for joining lightweight, untextured cottons such as lawn or dressmaking fabrics, and the flat, firm bond which is produced makes it unnecessary to match the grain precisely. Always follow the manufacturer's guidelines on heat settings for the iron, and use a pressing rather than a sliding motion so that the motif does not get stretched.

1 Trace the outline of the motif on to the paper side of the bonding web using a sharp pencil and cut out roughly. Do remember that the cut-out shape will be reversed, so if the motif is not symmetrical it will need to be drawn the other way round.

2 With the adhesive side down, place the bonding web on the wrong side of the appliqué fabric and use a warm, dry iron to fuse it in place (fig 1).

3 Cut out accurately around the outline, then peel off the backing paper (fig 2).

4 With the adhesive side down, position the motif on the background fabric. Cover with a damp cloth and iron it into place (fig 3).

Fabric adhesive

Special fabric adhesive is useful for fixing in place small appliqué shapes which are to be stitched down by machine or by hand, but it is not suitable for use with fine fabrics. This type of adhesive is available in liquid form or as a more convenient solid stick.

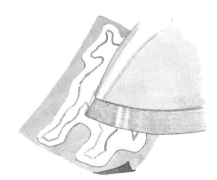

fig 1

fig 2

fig 3

Stitching the motifs

When stitching motifs by machine, work slowly and carefully, manipulating the fabric as it passes through the machine so that the foot is always parallel to the edge of the motif. Some machines are supplied with a transparent plastic foot which makes it easier to follow the needle. Always make sure you have a sharp needle fitted, as a blunt or damaged point can make the stitching irregular, and match the needle size to the weight of the fabric.

• Standard cotton or polyester sewing thread is suitable for straight or zigzag stitch, but machine embroidery thread produces a more lustrous satin stitch.
• Use the same colour thread top and bottom and try varying the tension; a slightly looser top thread gives a neat edge to a close satin stitch.
• When working on a lightweight background fabric there is a slight tendency for the stitching to pull, so the work may need to be reinforced using an iron-on interfacing.
• An embroidery hoop can also help to maintain an even surface when working on a small area. Mount the fabric so that it lies flat against the machine bed, with the right side upwards.

Straight stitch

An ordinary machine straight stitch can be used for sewing fabrics that do not fray, as the cut edges do not need to be hidden. Set to a slightly shorter length than for seaming – 7 stitches per cm (15 per in) – to give a more flexible line. Stitch just inside the motif and keep the needle a steady 3mm (⅛in) from the edge, using the presser foot as a guide.

Satin stitch and zigzag

The zigzag controls on the sewing machine can be set in several ways to produce a stitch that covers the cut edge of an appliqué motif. A narrow, open zigzag allows some of the fabric to show through, while a wide, closely set satin stitch is dense enough to hide the edge completely. Experiment on scraps of fabric to get the effect you want.

Points

For outside corners, work a line of zigzag to the furthest point, ending with the needle through the fabric on the right. Lift the presser foot, swing the work round, then continue to stitch along the next side (fig 4).

Inside corners

Work inside corners in the same way. Finish stitching so that the needle lies to the right before continuing along the next side (fig 5).

Curves

To work around a tight outside (convex) curve, pause every few stitches with the needle to the right of the presser foot. Adjust the angle of the fabric so that the foot remains parallel to the edge of the motif (fig 6). When stitching inside (concave) curves, pivot the work with the needle to the left of the foot.

Tapering

A neat, tapered finish can be achieved at both inside and outside corners by varying the stitch width to produce a fine point, as on the heart motif above left. This is done by slowly decreasing the stitch width as you approach the corner, pivoting the work, and then increasing the width on the second side.

fig 4

fig 5

fig 6

25

hearts edging

The heart is a symbol of romance and devotion throughout the world, and heart shapes were traditionally appliquéd on to marriage or baby quilts to signify affection. This festive border gives a new interpretation to the motif, and the combination of blue chambray, Provençal prints and gingham ribbon creates a bright, country feel. The heart shapes are edged by machine with a wide band of satin stitch. Alternatively, they could be secured with a decorative hand-embroidery stitch.

The repeat design allows the edging to be adapted to different lengths. A curtain wire runs along the top edge, so that the border can be used to decorate a window, shelf edge or mantelpiece; however, it would also make an attractive pelmet or an unusual edging for a roller blind.

You will need
For an edging approximately 20 x 143cm (8 x 56¼in):
0.5m (½yd) cotton chambray, 150cm (60in) wide
0.2m (¼yd) floral print cotton fabric, 114cm (45in) wide
30 x 45cm (12 x 18in) iron-on bonding web
3m (3¼yd) gingham ribbon, 3cm (1¼in) wide
Matching and toning sewing threads
1.5m (60in) curtain wire, with hooks and eyes for fixing

To prepare the appliqué
1 Using the actual size template on page 28, trace 13 hearts on to the paper side of the bonding web, and cut out roughly.
2 Look for interesting patterns within the floral fabric and select areas that will look effective when cut into a heart shape. Stripes can be positioned so that they run vertically or horizontally through the motif. Place the bonding web hearts, adhesive side down, on the wrong side of the fabric and fix in place using a dry iron. Cut out each heart around the pencil outline.

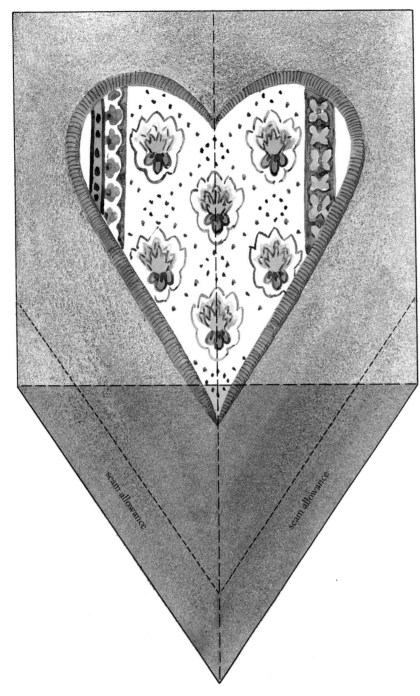

Using the heart shown here as a template, trace 13 heart motifs on to the paper side of bonding web. Use the shaded triangle to mark the zigzag edging.

To prepare the background

1 Using a ruler and set square, draw 2 long rectangles, each 22 x 145.5cm (8³/₄ x 57¹/₄in), on to the cotton chambray and cut out.

2 Mark the zigzag edging on to the lower long edge of one of the rectangles as follows. Trace the shaded triangle from the template and cut it out carefully. Mark in the dividing line. Then mark a line 12mm (½in) in from each side edge of the fabric. Pin the paper triangle at the bottom right-hand corner of the fabric rectangle, so that the long side sits on the bottom edge of the fabric and the dividing line of the triangle lies over the marked side line. Using a dressmaker's pen or chalk marking pencil, draw along the diagonal side of the triangle.

3 Unpin and move the paper cut-out to the left, so that it just touches the previous triangle, then mark the 2 diagonals. Continue in this way to the left-hand edge of the fabric (fig 1).

4 With the marked piece on top, pin the 2 fabric rectangles together carefully, placing the pins just inside the zigzag line. Cut out the triangles and remove the pins (fig 2).

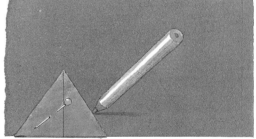

fig 1

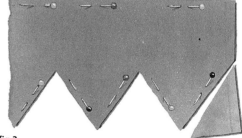

fig 2

To assemble the design

1 Peel the backing paper away from the cut-out hearts. Using the template on page 28 as a guide, position a heart on each point of one cotton chambray length. Fix them in place using a warm iron and a pressing cloth.

2 Thread the sewing machine with toning thread and set to a close zigzag (to be sure of a perfect finish, practise on an offcut of fabric first, adjusting the controls until you have a satisfactory satin stitch). Sew around each of the hearts to cover over the cut edges, tapering the stitch at the bottom point of the heart and in the dip at the top (fig 3). Secure the loose ends of thread on the wrong side and press lightly.

To make up

1 With the hearts facing inwards, pin the 2 cotton chambray lengths together, carefully matching the zigzag points and setting the pins at right angles to the edge. Thread the machine with matching sewing thread and, with a seam allowance of 12mm (½in), work straight stitch along the two short sides and the zigzag edge.

2 To give a sharp point to the triangles, snip off all the tips and trim back the surplus fabric on each side. At the valleys, clip the seam allowance almost to the stitching line (fig 4).

3 Turn the edging right side out and use the tip of your embroidery scissors to ease out each of the points gently. Finish the zigzag edge with a line of topstitching 3mm (⅛in) from the seam and press.

4 Pin the cut edges and stitch them together with a seam allowance of 12mm (½in). Trim back to 3mm (⅛in). Fold over an allowance of 12mm (½in) to the wrong side and press. Fold over a second time and press again. Pin the double fold in place and stitch along the lower edge to form a channel for the curtain wire.

5 Neaten the two ends of the gingham ribbon by making narrow double turnings and run a long gathering thread along one side. Draw it up so that the ribbon is the same length as the edging. Pin the ribbon in place over the channel stitching, and stitch down (fig 5). Thread the curtain wire through the channel and screw an eye into each end. Screw the hooks in position as required and hang up the edging.

fig 3

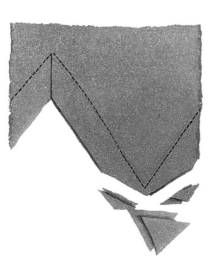

fig 4

fig 5

29

pattern-cut appliqué

Pattern-cut appliqué is a striking and deceptively simple technique, and various interpretations have developed in different cultures all over the world. Instead of building up a design from many smaller elements, just two layers of fabric are used, with the applied fabric cut into a decorative pattern before being stitched on to the background. The two main variations involve using this top layer to create either a positive or a negative image – in Hawaiian appliqué it is folded and cut into an elaborate motif, while in reverse appliqué areas of fabric are cut away to form the design.

Hawaiian appliqué

'Album' quilts, consisting of a variety of cut-out 'snowflake' patterns on a white cotton background, were made across America in the 1860s, but the technique reached its most elaborate interpretation in Hawaii, where the stylized naturalistic designs were based on the lush local surroundings of waterfalls, vines and palm trees.

The original Hawaiian quilts were cut from fine percale or sheeting fabric which had been dyed in strong colours. Plain white was usually chosen for the background, as this did not detract from the intricate design. Firmly woven cottons are still the best choice for both kinds of pattern-cut appliqué.

fig 1

fig 2

Cutting out designs

Instead of cutting the appliqué directly from fabric, a more accurate result is obtained by making a thin paper template which can then be drawn around. Spend some time experimenting with this method; unexpected and interesting motifs can be created by folding the paper in different ways and cutting out paper 'snowflakes' and other attractive patterns.

For example, a simple, symmetrical design such as a butterfly or tree can be made by folding just once, while snowflakes and other more complex motifs can be cut from a square piece of paper that has been folded into several segments. A fleur-de-lys motif, created by folding paper in this way, is shown above left.

Remember that over-complicated shapes will prove difficult to handle when transferred on to fabric, and that gentle curves and flowing lines are easier to neaten than sharp angles and geometric designs.

Assembling the appliqué

1 Cut out a square of layout paper to the size of the finished motif. Fold it carefully in half, then in quarters, and then diagonally into eighths. Draw on your design and cut it out (fig 1).

2 Unfold the pattern and smooth out the creases (you may need to use a cool iron). Pin the pattern template on to the right side of the appliqué fabric and draw around it using a dressmaker's pen or chalk marking pencil. Unpin the template.

3 Draw another line about 6mm (¼ in) outside the outline for the seam allowance. Cut out the shape around this second line, and clip the corners and curves using a pair of sharp scissors. Turn under the seam allowance and tack it in place (fig 2). Press lightly.

4 Mark diagonal guidelines on to the background fabric with lines of tacking (see page 17). Match up the neatened appliqué shape along these lines and pin, then tack it into place. Sew down with slip stitch or running stitch.

Reverse appliqué

The design in a multi-layered reverse appliqué is created by cutting away areas of the top fabrics to reveal the colours underneath. The most complex variation of the technique was developed among the people of the San Blas islands off the coast of Panama in Central America. Their *mola* work requires great expertise and can incorporate up to eight or nine different-coloured fabrics.

Two-layer reverse appliqué

Equally striking designs can be created from just two pieces of fabric using the method described below – choose a simple, bold outline so that the edges can be turned under and stitched easily. A quick alternative way of making a more complicated pattern is to trace the design for the top layer directly on to fusible bonding. Cut out the design carefully – you can experiment with more intricate shapes, as the bonding will support the fabric – and iron it on to the background fabric. The cut edges can then be concealed with decorative hand embroidery, couching or machine stitching (see the Decorative Stitching chapter for a selection of stitches).

Assembling the appliqué

1 Cut 2 pieces of fabric the same size and draw the design on to the top layer. Remember that this is, in effect, the background colour.

2 Tack the pieces together around the outside edge. Stitch a line of tacking around the motif outline, 12mm (½in) outside the drawn line and working through both layers (fig 3).

3 Cutting 6mm (¼in) inside the outline and using sharp embroidery scissors, cut through the top layer and remove the fabric within the motif (fig 4). Clip the interior angles and curves so that the seam allowance can be turned under.

4 Slip stitch the top layer of fabric to the background along the drawn line. Use the tip of your needle to push under the seam allowance as you work (fig 5).

More complicated designs, incorporating several colours, can be created following the same method. Cut through one, two or three layers to reveal the underlying fabrics, remembering that the further down the fabrics are, the simpler the shapes should be (fig 6). The colour that is used least should form the bottom layer.

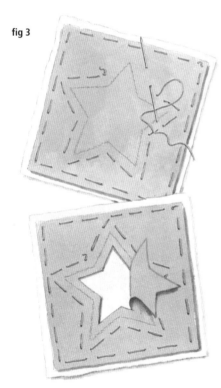

fig 3

fig 4

fig 5

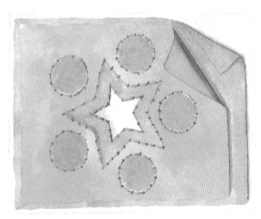

fig 6

snowflake cushions

This unusual trio of small cushions would be an ideal way in which to show off a collection of hatpins, or to display brooches on a dressing table. The three variations are made using the same basic method of pattern-cut appliqué. Subtly contrasting shades and textures of pure white cotton, jacquard-weave cotton and unbleached calico have been chosen to complement the simple, direct designs. The cushions could, however, be made up in any combination of fabrics to suit your own colour scheme. Additional templates are provided on pages 100–101.

You will need

For each cushion approximately 15cm (6in) square:
20 x 40cm (8 x 16in) white cotton fabric, to make each pad
Polyester toy filling
Cream stranded cotton
Matching sewing thread
For the square:
19 x 60cm (7½ x 24in) white cotton fabric
18cm (7in) square unbleached calico

72cm (28in) white cotton fringing, 2.5cm (1in) wide
For the butterfly:
18cm (7in) square white cotton fabric
20 x 50cm (8 x 21in) unbleached calico
4 cotton tassels, 10cm (4in) long
For the circle:
18cm (7in) square white jacquard-weave cotton fabric
18 x 50cm (7 x 20in) unbleached calico
72cm (28in) narrow looped braid edging

Square cushion

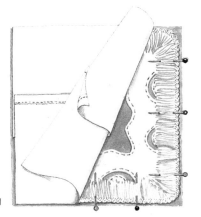

To prepare the cut-out

1 Enlarge the square motif on page 34 to 130% on a photocopier. Trace the outline and cut out the template. Cut out a 15cm (6in) square from white cotton fabric, pin the template to it and draw around the outside and inside edges. Add a 3mm (⅛in) seam allowance all round. Clip into the seam allowance around the curves and inside shapes, and finger press by turning the surplus fabric to the back and pressing it between your thumb and forefinger.

2 Cut out 9 circles 3cm (1⅛in) in diameter from white cotton fabric. Trace a smaller circle 1.5cm (⅝in) in diameter on to thin card. For each circle, run a gathering thread around the outside of the fabric. Place the card disc in the centre and draw up the thread tightly. Press from the right side and remove the card carefully (see page 16).

To work the appliqué

Cut out a 19cm (7½in) square from unbleached calico and place the appliqué shape in the centre. Pin, then tack in place. Tack one circle in the centre, then arrange 2 on each side. Sew down the

shapes with running stitch, using a single strand of cream stranded cotton. Press lightly from the right side, using a pressing cloth.

To make up

1 Pin the white cotton fringing around the edge of the right side of the cushion front, so that it faces inwards.
2 Cut out 2 rectangles, each 12 x 19cm (5 x 7½in), from white cotton fabric for the cushion back. Fold under and hem one long side of each piece. Place the back pieces face down on either side of the appliqué so that the hemmed edges overlap (fig 1), and pin in position.
3 Machine stitch all the way around the cushion cover, 12mm (½in) from the cut edges. Clip the surplus fabric from the corners and turn right side out.

To make the cushion pad

Cut out 2 18cm (7in) squares of white cotton fabric and stitch them together with a seam allowance of 12mm (½in). Leave a small gap on one side, and turn right side out. Stuff with polyester toy filling, then slip stitch the gap closed. Insert the pad into the cushion cover.

Butterfly cushion

fig 1

To prepare the cut-out

1 Enlarge the butterfly motif to 130% on a photocopier. Trace and cut out. Cut out a 18cm (7in) square from white cotton fabric, pin the template to it and draw around the edges. Add a 3mm (⅛ in) seam allowance all round. Cut out, carefully snipping away the fabric from within the wing markings.

2 Clip into the seam allowance around the curves and inside shapes so that the appliqué will lie flat and finger press (see instructions for the Square cushion).

To work the appliqué

1 Cut out a 20cm (8in) square from unbleached calico and place the butterfly in the centre. Pin, then tack in place. Sew down with running stitch, using a single strand of cream stranded cotton. Press lightly from the right side, using a pressing cloth. Embroider the antennae on to the cushion front with backstitch and French knots, using cream stranded cotton, then work French knots around the wing markings.

To make up

1 Cut out 2 rectangles, each measuring 15 x 20cm (6 x 8in), from unbleached calico for the cushion back. Fold under and hem one long side of each piece. Turn the cushion front face up. Place the back pieces face down on either side of the appliqué so that the hemmed edges overlap, and pin in position.

2 Machine stitch all the way around the cushion, 12mm (½in) from the cut edges. Leave a 2cm (¾in) gap in the stitching at each corner ready for inserting the tassels (fig 1).

3 Turn the cushion cover right side out. Fold under the cut edges at each of the corner gaps, then push the top of the first tassel into one of these spaces. Secure the tassel firmly in position with hand stitching. Repeat to secure the other 3 tassels.

To make the cushion pad

Follow the instructions for the Square cushion on page 32, using 2 19cm (7½in) squares of white cotton fabric.

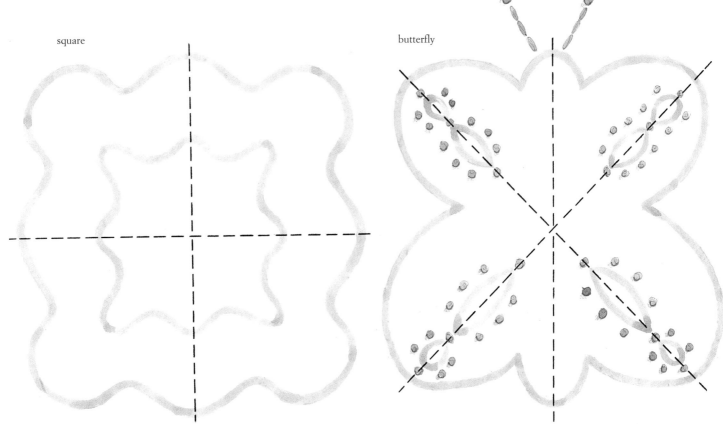

square

butterfly

Enlarge the Square, Butterfly and Circle motifs to 130% on a photocopier. Add a 3mm (⅛in) seam allowance all round when drawing on to the fabric.

Circle cushion

To prepare the cut-out

1 Enlarge the circle motif to 130% on a photocopier. Trace and cut out. Cut out a 15cm (6in) square from unbleached calico, pin the template to it, and draw around it. Add a 3mm (⅛in) seam allowance all around. Using embroidery scissors, cut out around the main outline, then carefully snip away the fabric within the circle and 4 tear-shaped holes.

2 Snip carefully around the seam allowance. Using the ends of the blades, make cuts about 3mm (⅛in) deep into the curves and clip the corners (fig 1). Clip the central circle and 4 tear-shapes in the same way, and finger press (see instructions for the Square Cushion).

To work the appliqué

Cut out a 18cm (7in) square from white jacquard-weave cotton fabric and place the cut-out in the centre. Pin, then tack in place. Sew down with small, neat running stitches, using a single strand of cream stranded cotton (fig 2). Work close to the turned-under edge, pushing the allowance under with the tip of the needle as necessary. When the stitching is complete, press lightly from the right side using a pressing cloth.

To make up

1 Cut 4 18cm (7in) lengths of looped braid edging. Pin and tack one length along each side, so that they face inwards (fig 3).

2 Cut out 2 rectangles, each 12 x 18cm (5 x 7in), from unbleached calico for the cushion back. Fold under and hem one long side of each piece. Turn the cushion front face upwards. Place the back pieces face down on either side of the appliqué, so that the hemmed edges overlap. Pin in position.

3 Machine stitch all the way around the cushion, 12mm (½in) from the cut edges, catching in the looped braid. Clip surplus fabric from the corners and turn the cushion cover right side out.

To make the cushion pad

Follow the instructions for the Square cushion on page 32, using 2 17cm (6¾in) squares of white cotton fabric.

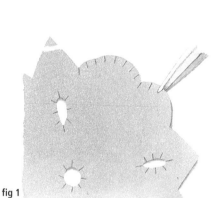

fig 1

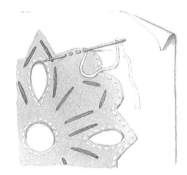

fig 2

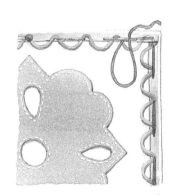

fig 3

circle

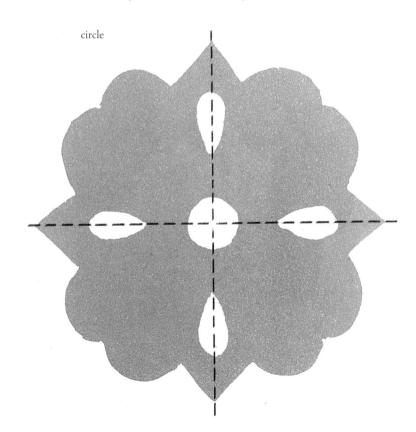

Decorative stitching

Hand embroidery has long been combined with appliqué techniques to produce a wealth of varied texture, colour and surface decoration. The turned-edge method of sewing down shapes deliberately uses an invisible slip stitch so that the stitching is unobtrusive. However, when a more elaborate stitch is chosen to secure a motif, the embroidery becomes part of the overall design. The particular threads and stitches selected may complement or contrast with the appliquéd fabrics. Stitching can also be used to embellish the appliqué shapes, to 'draw in' details or to highlight areas of a printed fabric. Machine embroidery stitches can be explored in the same way to add visual interest to appliqué designs.

This chapter provides a useful library of decorative hand stitches suitable for appliqué, while the projects illustrate some of the varied uses of both hand and machine embroidery.

embroidering on appliqué

There is a vast, historic 'language' of stitches available to the embroiderer, which can be interpreted to suit any purpose. You may want to create a densely ornamented surface decorated with a range of complex stitches, or, at the other extreme, simply wish to sew around a single motif in a contrasting colour. Both are perfectly possible – entire reference books have been devoted to fancy stitchery and there are many old and new stitch directories available which can prove a fascinating and endless source of inspiration. The stitch library on pages 39–41 describes a range of useful stitches for combining with appliqué techniques. It is divided into three groups: outline, edging and filling stitches.

Hand embroidery

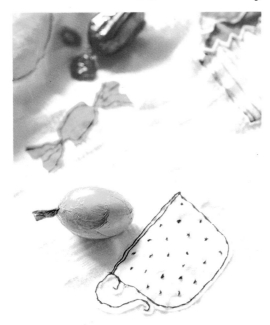

The addition of embroidered effects using decorative stitches and lustrous threads can be used to enhance a piece of appliqué in a variety of ways:

• To hold down the motifs instead of using slip stitch. This can be done using a matching thread for a subtle, textured effect, or with a brightly contrasting colour to draw attention to the shape of the motif itself.
• To conceal the edges of a motif by working a line of stitching over the join. This is also a good way to disguise the cut edges of a motif that has been attached with iron-on bonding web (see page 24).
• To 'draw in' details in a graphic way, either on plain shapes or to emphasize patterned areas within a printed fabric. For example, stitches can be used to indicate the veins on a leaf or even to add spikes to a cactus.

Learning the stitches

Making a traditional sampler is still the best way of learning new embroidery stitches. This will not only produce a useful source for future reference, but will help you get the feel of working evenly and rhythmically. Take time to try some of the stitches shown in the stitch library on the following three pages. In addition, work out some new variations

of your own, and practice embroidering with different types and shades of thread. Beads, buttons and sequins can all be incorporated with your stitching.

Starting and finishing

There are not many rules for hand embroidery, but a few points should be borne in mind while stitching to help give your work a professional finish.
• Never work with a thread longer than 45cm (18in). A longer thread will twist and become frayed and worn as it passes through the fabric, giving an untidy look to the stitches.
• Choose a needle that can be threaded easily and that will pass through the layers of fabric without being tugged. Too small a needle is difficult to work with and can damage the thread.
• Most threads can be secured on the wrong side with a tight knot and finished off with a small double stitch worked through the back of the preceding stitches.
• Your stitches should always be of a regular size and equally spaced. Do not pull the thread too tightly or they will become distorted.

Machine embroidery

The decorative qualities of machine stitches should not be ignored. As well as the possibilities for free embroidery, worked with the feed dogs lowered or covered, all swing-needle machines have a series of pre-programmed embroidery stitches. With imagination, these can be used to provide an attractive and hardwearing form of decoration for machine-appliquéd motifs.

Outline stitches

This group of stitches can be used to hold motifs in place on the background fabric, as well as to add ornament. They are usually worked on turned-edge appliqué to add interest to the plain edge, or on non-fray fabrics such as felt.

Backstitch

Backstitch is worked from right to left and produces a solid line. Make a row of small stitches, taking the needle back to the end of the previous stitch each time.

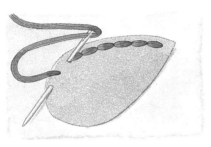

Chain stitch

This makes a flexible, linked line. Loop the thread under the needle as you pull it through. Insert the needle where it last emerged to begin the next chain.

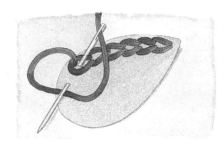

Stem stitch

Also known as crewel stitch, stem stitch is worked from left to right or bottom to top, with the needle always brought up on the left side of the previous stitch.

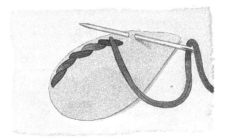

Whipped running stitch

The twisted cord-like appearance of this stitch is created by weaving a second thread under and over a foundation line of running stitch (see page 17).

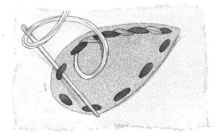

Coral stitch

This stitch forms an irregular, textured outline. Using the tip of the needle, pick up a few threads at right angles to the stitching line, looping the thread around the needle as shown.

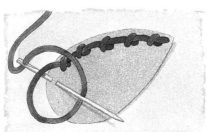

Couching

This technique consists of securing one thread with small stitches of another. Hold the thicker thread around the motif and catch it down with straight stitches of the thinner thread.

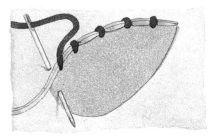

Edging stitches

All the stitches in this group can be worked so that they mask the cut or turned edge of an appliquéd motif. If the thread covers the edge completely, there is no need to add an extra seam allowance to the motif.

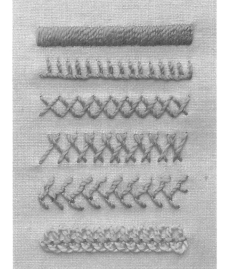

Satin stitch
This stitch has a smooth finish, which works well with a shiny thread. The stitches are all worked in the same direction and lie evenly, side by side.

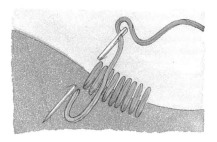

Blanket stitch
Traditionally associated with appliqué, this adaptable stitch is worked from left to right, with the needle always kept at right angles to the edge of the motif.

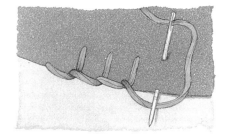

Cross stitch
Usually worked as a counted-thread stitch, cross stitch can be used to give an interesting edge to a shape. The top stitches should lie in the same direction.

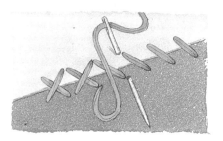

Herringbone stitch
This stitch forms a wide, decorative band of regular overlapping stitches. Work diagonal stitches in alternate directions, each one separated by a backstitch.

Feather stitch
Feather stitch creates an attractive open effect which covers the edges of appliquéd shapes well. Work alternate diagonal stitches, with the thread below the needle to form the loops.

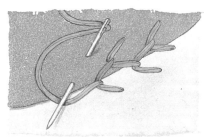

Pekinese stitch
This stitch gives a dense, braid-like border to a motif. Make a foundation row of backstitches and then pass a second thread through this, on the surface only, in overlapping loops.

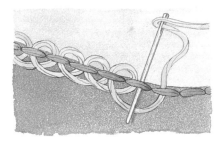

Filling stitches

These detached stitches are used to fill in clearly defined areas, so are an ideal way to add texture and colour to plain appliqué shapes. Some, such as French knots, can be worked singly or in rows.

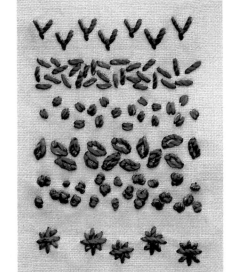

Fly stitch

For fly stitch, bring the thread through, then make a downwards diagonal stitch from right to left, catching the thread down with a short straight stitch.

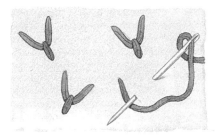

Straight stitch

This simple stitch can either be worked regularly in neat horizontal and vertical rows, or so that the stitches all lie randomly at different angles.

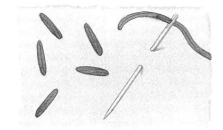

Seed stitch

This little stitch is made by working pairs of short, parallel backstitches which are scattered haphazardly across the surface of the motif.

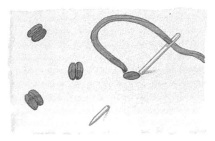

Detached chain stitch

Also called lazy daisy stitch, this variation on chain stitch is constructed in the same way as fly stitch, but with the stitch closed at the top to form a loop.

French knots

Bring the thread through and, keeping it taut with your thumb, twist the needle around it twice. Insert the needle back through the fabric close to the starting point and draw through to form a knot.

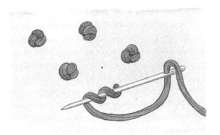

Double cross stitch

This double stitch is made up of two simple cross stitches, worked at an angle to each other to create a star shape. The size of the top cross can be varied to form a square or diamond-shaped stitch.

leaf table linen

Simple stitches worked in bright embroidery threads are combined here with bold leaf shapes cut from vibrant cotton fabrics to give a Matisse-like quality to a striking set of linen, which would bring the colours of summer to any table. Make individual placemats, or join several pieces of fabric together to create a co-ordinating tablecloth. You may wish to choose from the various leaf templates provided here and on pages 102–103, or you could collect your own selection of leaves to make a lasting souvenir of a country walk, perhaps embroidering on the date or the name of the place where you found them to remind you of a special day.

You will need
*For each placemat 30 x 45cm
(12 x 18in):*
35 x 50cm (14 x 20in) brightly coloured heavyweight cotton fabric
20 x 30cm (8 x 12in) contrasting lighter-weight cotton fabric
Contrasting fine and medium pearl cottons
Selection of leaves (optional)

*For a tablecloth 71 x 107cm
(28 x 42in):*
6 38cm (15in) squares different-coloured heavyweight cotton fabrics
6 20 x 30cm (8 x 12in) pieces different-coloured lightweight cotton fabrics
Contrasting stranded cottons and fine and medium pearl cottons
Matching sewing threads
2.5m (3 yd) ricrac braid

Placemats

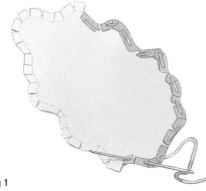

To make the basic mat
1 Cut out a rectangle 35 x 50cm (14 x 20in) from heavyweight cotton fabric. Turn under a 12mm (½in) double hem around the edge, press with a hot iron and pin the layers together.
2 Secure the hem with a line of French knots, worked approximately 2–3cm (1in) apart. Use a medium pearl cotton in a bright colour, so that the stitches will stand out against the background.

To prepare the appliqué
1 Enlarge the templates on pages 44–45 to 156% on a photocopier; enlarge the templates on pages 102–103 as instructed. Draw around the cut-out leaves on to lighter-weight cotton fabric. Alternatively, you could trace around a real leaf – you may have to simplify a complicated edge. Add a seam allowance of 6mm (¼in) all round and cut out.
2 Snip up to the drawn line at the points and curves, then fold back and tack down the seam allowance with small, neat stitches (fig 1). Arrange the leaves on the mat, using the templates as a guide if necessary, and pin in place.

To embroider the motifs
1 With a contrasting fine thread, stitch down the leaves with a regular running stitch (fig 2). Mark the stems using a dressmaker's pen and sew over the drawn lines with several rows of long backstitches in pearl cotton.
2 Draw the veins on the back of each leaf. Embroider them with straight stitches, using a contrasting fine thread (fig 3). If you wish, write the name of the tree in the bottom right corner and work over the letters with backstitch.

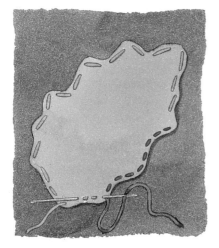

fig 2   fig 3

Tablecloth

To work the appliqué

Appliqué a different leaf pattern on to each of the squares of heavyweight cotton fabric, following the instructions for the placemat.

To make up

1 Arrange the appliquéd squares in 2 rows of 3, so that the colours balance well. Pin each row together, then sew by hand with slip stitch or by machine using a toning sewing thread, with a seam allowance of 12mm (½ in). Press the allowances to one side, then pin the 2 rows together, matching the joins carefully. Press.

2 Stitch ricrac braid over the seams to conceal the joins, using a matching sewing thread. Turn under a narrow double hem all round, then press and pin in place. Work French knots as for the placemats to keep the hem in place, using a different colour of pearl cotton for each square.

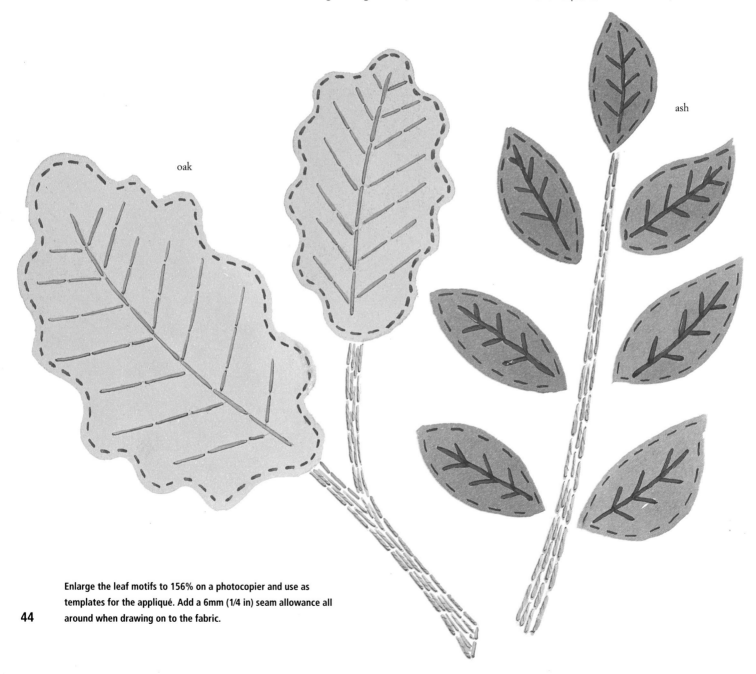

oak

ash

Enlarge the leaf motifs to 156% on a photocopier and use as templates for the appliqué. Add a 6mm (1/4 in) seam allowance all around when drawing on to the fabric.

maple

willow

kitchen curtains

The familiar outline of the kitchen teapot forms the centrepiece of these fabric panels. Along with the other tea-table motifs, it is cut from specially painted cotton fabric which does not fray. The motifs are sewn in simple backstitch to resemble a drawn line. The stitchery is used both to secure the appliqué to the background fabric and to indicate pattern details, giving a lively, graphic quality to the shapes. This is an adaptable project – the randomly scattered motifs could be arranged to fit any size of panel and painted in colours to match your own colour scheme.

You will need

2 lengths self-check textured white fabric to fit your window or cupboard
90 x 50cm (36 x 20in) white cotton fabric, such as sheeting
Fabric paints in white, blue, yellow, green, red and orange, or selection of your choice
Paintbrush
Fabric glue
Dark blue stranded cotton
Curtain header tape or curtain wire

To prepare the appliqué

1 Paint pieces of white cotton fabric for the cut-out shapes, mixing the fabric paints to achieve the desired shades. Allow at least 25 x 40cm (10 x 16in) in orange; 25cm (10in) square in yellow, blue, cream and white; 25 x 10cm (10 x 4in) in green, red and tan. It is a good idea to have extra fabric to work with, and you may wish to experiment with the paint to produce textured, sponged-type patterns. Allow the paint to dry, then press to fix the colour, following the manufacturer's instructions.

2 Enlarge the templates shown on pages 48 and 49 to 110% on a photocopier. Cut out the motifs carefully. The cake is made up of 4 separate elements: the cherry, the icing, the cake and its paper case. Trace off individual templates for each of these elements. In the same way, draw separate templates for the leaves, flower and flower centre that decorate the jug.

3 Draw directly around the paper patterns on to the painted fabric using a

fig 1

soft pencil (fig 1). Cut out the motifs around this outline, removing the spare fabric from within the handles carefully. Reverse the templates for some of the cups so that you have a range of shapes and sizes. To make the panels as shown, you will need to cut out:

orange: 2 sugar bowls, 2 teapots (one facing each way), 2 cups, 1 flower for jug
yellow: 5 sweets, 2 cups, 1 flower centre
blue: 4 sweets, 2 cups
cream: 1 cup, 5 icing tops, 1 spoon, 1 fork
white: 5 cake paper cases, 1 jug
green: 6 sweets, 2 leaves
red: 24 cherries
tan: 5 cakes

To assemble the design

1 Fold the lengths of textured fabric in half lengthways and widthways to find the centre, and place one of the teapots in the middle of each. Lay the pieces side by side on a flat surface and arrange the other motifs around the teapots to form a balanced layout. You may wish to refer to the photograph as a guide, or prefer to make your own design. When you are satisfied with the arrangement, use a small amount of fabric glue to hold each of the shapes in place.

2 Arrange each cake so that the sponge goes down first, with the icing and the paper case overlapping it at top and bottom. Each cake is topped with a cherry. Fix the flower on the milk jug with one leaf on either side. The yellow circle is glued in the flower centre.

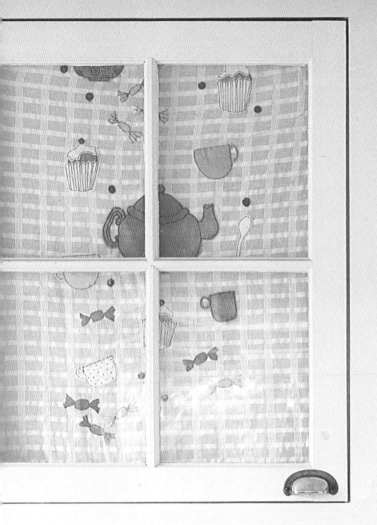

To embroider the motifs

1 The motifs are all held down with backstitch, which is also used to indicate the details on the motifs. Sew with a single thread of dark blue stranded cotton for a fine line. Make the stitches fairly large and do not worry if they are not perfectly regular – this will give an informal air to the stitchery. Follow the lines on the templates as a guide to where the details need to be filled in.
2 The spotted design on the white teacup is indicated with seed stitch and the concentric circles on the sugar bowl are worked in backstitch (fig 2). The folds on the cake paper case are worked with long, single straight stitches (fig 3).

To finish

Make a double hem of 12mm (½ in) along each side and the bottom edge of both curtain panels, mitring the corners. They can be finished off with a curtain header tape or a curtain wire threaded through a channel at the top, depending on where they are to hang.

fig 2

fig 3

Enlarge the motifs to 110% on a photocopier and use as templates for the appliqué.

workbag, housewife & needlebook

A special container for needlework tools and materials is essential for everyone who enjoys sewing. This festive set of matching workbag, needlebook and old-fashioned 'housewife' will ensure that your equipment is always stored safely in the same place, and can be carried with you wherever you are working.

The needlebook, with its felt 'pages', is the best way to keep your needles to hand, as they are liable to get lost inside a pincushion, while a roll-up housewife has long been a favourite method of safeguarding scissors, ruler, tailor's chalk and other essentials. The roomy base of the workbag is made from felt-covered card trimmed with harlequin diamonds and embroidered circles, in colours chosen to co-ordinate with the floral print of the drawstring top.

Housewife

You will need

Felt as follows:

    30 x 45cm (12 x 18in) dark blue
    15 x 15cm (6 x 6in) pink
    15 x 7.5cm (6 x 3in) green
    15 x 7.5cm (6 x 3in) white

Matching dark blue, pink and green
    stranded cottons

To make the cover

1 From dark blue felt cut out 2 main pieces, each 20 x 30cm (8 x 12in). Enlarge the templates for the petals and the flower centre on page 53 to 143% on a photocopier. Cut out from felt: 6 white, 4 green and 4 pink outer petals; 7 green and 7 pink inner petals; 1 white and 1 pink flower centre.

2 Arrange the outer petals to form 2 flower shapes at the edge of one of the main pieces. Make a 6-petalled white flower and an 8-petalled flower with alternate green and pink petals, overlapping some of them. Pin, then blanket stitch in place, using contrasting pink stranded cotton for the white petals and dark blue for the other flower.

3 Pin the inner petals on to the flowers, alternating pink with green. Sew down with straight stitches worked at right angles to the edges of the shapes, using dark blue stranded cotton. Attach the pink flower centre to the white flower and the white flower centre to the other flower with blanket stitch, using green stranded cotton. Decorate with a few contrasting French knots.

To make the inside

1 Enlarge the patterns for the pockets and pencil holder on page 53 to 143% on a photocopier. Cut out the shorter pocket (1) in green felt, the scissor pocket (2) and the taller pocket (4) in pink felt, and the pencil holder (3) in white felt. Pin these pieces in place on the second main piece.

2 Sew down the pockets with blanket stitch, using a contrasting stranded cotton for each felt colour. Secure the ends of the pencil holder 6.5cm (2½in) apart with blanket stitch, then sew 3 vertical lines of running stitch to divide it into 4 loops (fig 1).

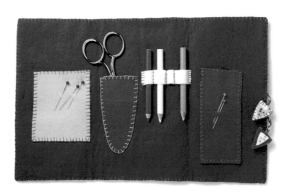

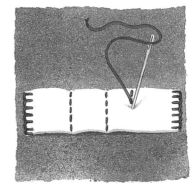

fig 1

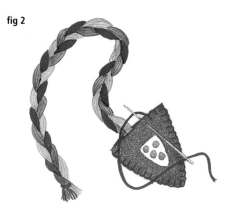

fig 2

To make the fastening

1 Cut 3 30cm (12in) lengths from each of the 3 coloured stranded cottons to make the tie cord. Knot tightly at one end and plait them together. Tie the other end in a knot and trim the loose ends.

2 Enlarge the templates on page 53 to 143% on a photocopier and cut out one large and one small triangular tab from each of the 4 different-coloured felts. Choosing contrasting colours, secure the inner triangles in place on the larger triangles with 4 French knots.

3 Join 2 of the triangles together along the long sides with blanket stitch and slip this over one of the knotted ends of the tie cord. Sew the third side together with blanket stitch, securing the tie cord in

place (fig 2). Make the other tab in the same way and secure it over the other knotted end of the tie cord. Fold the cover into thirds and sew the tie cord in place at its centre, half-way along the folded edge.

4 Enlarge the button templates on page 53 to 143% on a photocopier and cut a large pink and a smaller green circle from felt. Join the circles with a few dark blue French knots and stitch on to the appliquéd side of the cover in line with the tie.

To finish

Pin the inside piece to the wrong side of the cover. Join them together around the outer edge with blanket stitch worked in pink stranded cotton.

Needlebook

You will need

Felt as follows:
- 15 x 18cm (6 x 7in) dark blue
- 15 x 23cm (6 x 9in) green
- 15cm (6in) square pink

Matching dark blue, green and pink stranded cottons

Pinking shears

To cut out

1 Cut out a rectangle of dark blue felt 12.5 x 18cm (5 x 7in) for the main cover. Make the inner pages from one rectangle of pink felt 10 x 15cm (4 x 6in), and one rectangle of green 9 x 12.5cm (3½ x 5in). Cut out the pages using pinking shears.

2 Enlarge the templates on page 53 to

143% on a photocopier. Trace the zigzag panel and use to cut out the motif from green felt. Trace the 2 diamond-shaped petals and circular flower centre. Cut out 4 pink and 4 dark blue petals from both the large and small templates, and 2 green flower centres.

To make the cover

1 Lay the 8 larger petals in place on the right-hand side of the green zigzag panel. Place them in a flower shape and pin in place, alternating the pink and blue petals and overlapping them slightly as you go around. Blanket stitch in place using green stranded cotton. Stitch as far around each petal as you can.

2 Sew the green flower centre on to the middle of the flower so that it conceals the ends of the petals. Use blanket stitch, worked in pink stranded cotton ·for this (fig 1).

3 On the left-hand side of the background piece, work the smaller flower in the same way.

4 Using dark blue stranded cotton, work a sprinkling of evenly spaced French knots across the background, and finish off the flower centres by working 3 knots on each.

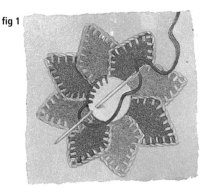

fig 1

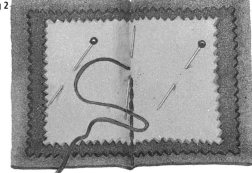

fig 2

Needlebook

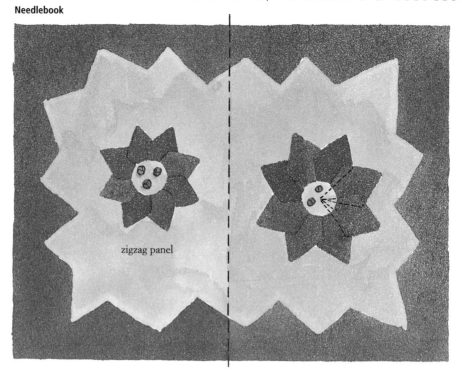

zigzag panel

5 Tack the appliquéd piece in place on the main cover. Sew it down all around the outer edge with blanket stitch, using pink stranded cotton. Try not to take the needle right through the blue felt background, so that the stitches do not show on the wrong side.

To make up
Lay the 2 inner pages inside the main cover of the needlebook and pin in place. Fold the cover in half to find the exact centre line then, using pink stranded cotton, backstitch the 3 layers together along the spine (fig 2).

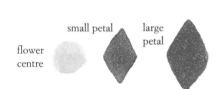

flower centre

small petal

large petal

Enlarge all the templates to 143% on a photocopier.

Housewife

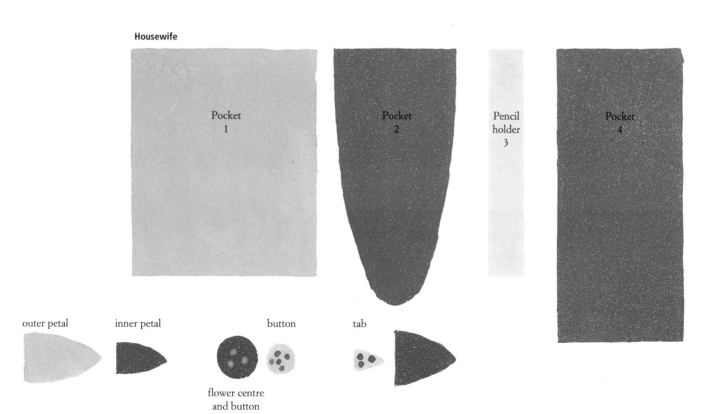

Pocket 1

Pocket 2

Pencil holder 3

Pocket 4

outer petal

inner petal

button

tab

flower centre and button

53

Workbag

Enlarge the templates to 143 % on a photocopier.

You will need

Felt as follows:
    40 x 71cm (16 x 28in) dark blue
    25cm (10in) square green
    25cm (10in) square pink
Matching dark blue, pink and green stranded cottons
25 x 69cm (10 x 27in) cotton fabric with small-scale floral print
61 x 69cm (24 x 27in) pink cotton fabric, for lining
Sewing thread to match cotton fabrics
A2 sheet medium-weight card
Masking tape
Craft glue
Metal ruler
Craft knife
Safety pin

To make the drum

1 Using a set square, draw a rectangle 15 x 66cm (6 x 26in) on to medium-weight card. Using a pair of compasses, draw a circle with a radius of 11.5cm (4½in). This will be the base. Draw a circle with a radius of 10cm (4in) inside the main circle. Cut out both shapes accurately using a craft knife.

2 Score along the outline of the inner circle, then snip around the outer edge to form tabs. Bend these upwards. Curve the rectangle into a cylinder, overlapping the edges by 12mm (½in). Glue the edges together using craft glue and tape down with masking tape. Spread a thin layer of glue on the outside of the tabs and fit the cylinder over the base (fig 1). Secure with extra masking tape if necessary.

To cover the drum

1 Cut out a rectangle 16.5 x 68cm (6½ x 26½in) from dark blue felt. This is decorated before being glued to the card drum.

2 Enlarge the 2 circle templates given below left to 143% on a photocopier. Cut out from felt 7 green and 7 pink outer circles, and 7 dark blue, 4 pink and 3 green inner circles. Pin them together in pairs and arrange along the rectangle of dark blue felt. Tack in position, then stitch down using contrasting stranded cottons. Use either blanket stitch, a scattering of French knots or double cross stitch.

3 Spread a light coat of glue over the drum and wrap the appliquéd felt around it. Fold a 12mm (½in) allowance over the top edge and glue down. Allow an overlap of 12mm (½in) at the side. To secure the side seam, work a line of blanket stitch over the cut edge, using pink stranded cotton. Draw a circle with a radius of 10cm (4in) on to a piece of paper, cut out and use as a template to cut out a circle of dark blue felt. Glue to the drum base. Using pink stranded cotton, sew a line of decorative blanket stitch around the bottom edge (fig 2).

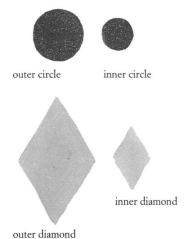

outer circle   inner circle

outer diamond

inner diamond

fig 1

fig 2

To make the gathered top

1 Cut out a circle with a radius of 11.5cm (4½in) from pink cotton fabric, using a paper template as a guide as before. Cut out a rectangle 38 x 69cm (15 x 27in) from the same fabric. With right sides facing, fold the rectangle in half and sew the 2 short edges together with a seam allowance of 12mm (½in). Press the seam open. With right sides together, pin the circle to the lower edge of this cylinder, and sew around the outside edge.

2 Cut out a rectangle 25 x 69cm (10 x 27in) from floral-print cotton fabric. With right sides facing, join the 2 short edges, leaving a 12mm (½in) seam allowance. Press the seam open, then pin to the open top edge of the lining, right sides together. Sew the 2 workbag pieces together with a 12mm (½in) seam allowance to form a long duffle-bag shape (fig 3).

3 Turn the floral fabric to the right side and press the folded seam. Cut out a 66cm (26in) strip of dark blue felt, 2cm (¾in) wide, to form the drawstring channel. Turn under 6mm (¼in) at each short end and pin the strip around the top edge, 4cm (1½in) from the fold. Stitch down along both long edges with blanket stitch, using green stranded cotton (fig 4).

To make up

1 Place the fabric top inside the covered drum and pin the cut edge of the floral fabric to the inside of the rim. Sew firmly in place, stitching through the lining, the floral fabric and the felt. The diamond trim will conceal this join.

2 Enlarge the inner and outer diamond templates on page 54 to 143% on a photocopier, and cut out from felt 10 pink and 10 green outer diamonds, and 20 dark blue inner diamonds. Join them in pairs with a few French knots using pink stranded cotton. Overstitch around the outer edges in a contrasting colour – green for the pink diamonds and dark blue for the green.

3 Sew the diamonds around the rim, securing them to the felt with a few overstitches on either side, so that the top and bottom points are left free. Alternate the colours for a harlequin effect.

4 Make the drawstring cord by plaiting together 3 60cm (24in) strands of each colour of stranded cotton. Knot firmly at each end, then fasten one end to a safety pin. Thread this through the drawstring channel.

5 For the decorative tabs that cover the ends of the cord, cut out 2 inner and 2 outer diamonds each in dark blue and again in green felt. Join them together as before with French knots, using pink stranded cotton, then pin in pairs on either side of the cord knots. Join together with blanket stitch worked in pink stranded cotton.

fig 3

fig 4

alphabet quilt

This quilt, which could also be used as a nursery hanging or play mat, was inspired by traditional teaching quilts, made to introduce the alphabet to small children in an informal way. The favourite nineteenth-century colour scheme of turkey red on white gives the quilt a fresh appeal.

The quilt is practical as well as decorative: the fabrics used – cotton sheeting, check homespun and iron-on polyester wadding – are all washable. The appliqué is finished with machine zigzag, so will withstand hard wear. The alphabet, numerals and some extra motifs are given on pages 104–105 and pages 108–109.

You will need

For a finished play mat 75cm (30in) square:

75cm (30in) square white cotton fabric, such as sheeting

75cm (30in) dark red cotton fabric of similar weight, 115cm (45in) wide

40 x 80cm (16 x 32in) red-and-white check cotton fabric, such as homespun

1.4m (1½yd) iron-on bonding web, 44cm (17in) wide

75cm (30in) square lightweight iron-on polyester wadding

Red and white sewing threads

To prepare the motifs

1 Enlarge the templates for the motifs on pages 58 and 59 to 154% on a photocopier; enlarge the letters on pages 108–109 as instructed. Cut out and turn face downwards. Trace the reversed outlines on to the paper side of the iron-on bonding web, leaving at least 12mm (½in) between them. To make the quilt as illustrated, you will need the entire capital and lower-case alphabets, 4 stars, 2 shoes, 2 socks, bucket and spade, scissors, bird, camel, giraffe, rattle, spoon and fork.

2 Cut out the letters and motifs roughly. Cut out a 75cm (30in) square from dark red cotton fabric to make the backing, and use the remainder of this fabric for

the motifs. Place the motifs adhesive side down on the fabric, following the grain where possible, and fix them in place using a dry iron. Trim accurately around the outline of each shape.

To prepare the background

1 Cut out a 45cm (17½in) square from paper to act as a template for marking the centre panel. Fold it in half vertically, horizontally and diagonally to find the

centre. Fold the square of white cotton fabric in the same way, pressing each fold lightly. Use these creases as a guideline to pin the paper square to the centre of the fabric. Mark around the 4 sides of the square using a chalk marking pencil and unpin the paper (fig 1).

2 Using a ruler, measure a line 4cm (1½ in) outside each side of the square and draw this in as a guide for placing the capital letters (fig 2).

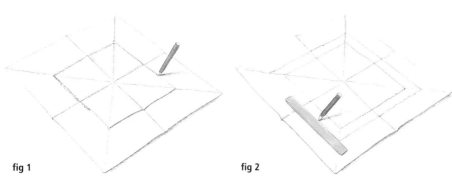

fig 1   fig 2

Placement diagram for the quilt

To position the motifs

1 Sort out the capital letters into 4 groups: A–F, G–M, N–T and U–Z. Arrange one group along each side of the marked square, making sure that the letters are evenly spaced and placed in alphabetical order. Iron down one letter at a time, removing its backing paper and pressing it carefully in place. Fix a star motif in each corner to complete the border design.

2 The lower-case letters and motifs are scattered within the centre panel. You can use the placement diagram on the left as a guide or make your own arrangement. Spend time finding a satisfactory layout. Ensure that the outer shapes all butt against the square outline to define the centre panel. Iron each of the motifs into place in the same way as for the alphabet.

To stitch the motifs

1 Using white sewing thread, work the machine-embroidered details. The automatic patterns vary between machine models, so experiment to find stitches that you like.

The motifs on the quilt illustrated are decorated as follows. The tops of the socks are indicated with 3 parallel bands of stitching. The rattle is decorated with 2 lines across the centre, and there are 3 straight-stitch stars on the bucket. A narrow zigzag is used on the spade and for the bird's wing. Its eye, and those of the camel and giraffe, are marked with satin stitch. The inside line on the shoes is also zigzagged, and the sunburst motif and buttons are in satin stitch. Use a needle to pass all the loose ends of thread through to the back of the work and tie off securely.

2 Thread the machine with red sewing thread and set the controls to a narrow zigzag. Stitch around the outside of each shape to cover the cut edges. Work slowly and carefully, especially around the curves, and pivot the work at the corners to give a neat outline (see page 25). Finish off all the loose ends and press the quilt top.

To make up

1 Following the manufacturer's instructions, iron the wadding to the back of the appliquéd square. Tack the dark red fabric backing in place around the 4 edges.

2 Cut the checked cotton fabric into 4 strips, each 10 x 80cm (4 x 32in), to make the bindings for the edges. Press each strip in half lengthways, then press under a seam allowance of 12mm (½in) along both sides of each strip. Bind the cut edges with these strips, neatening each corner by trimming and turning under the cut edges, and slip stitching the outside edge.

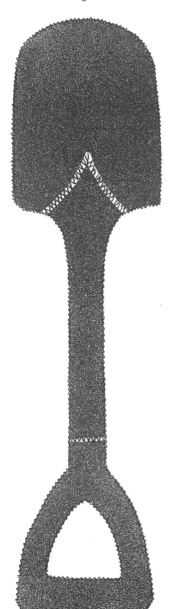

Enlarge the motifs to 154% on a photocopier and use as templates for the appliqué.

59

animal scarves

Appliqué is very adaptable and can be used easily to decorate a wide range of ready-made items. These standard woollen scarves have been transformed into distinctive and desirable accessories by adding animal motifs cut from felt. The hart and deer lend a baronial air to traditional tartan, while the brightly coloured dogs stand out from their purple background.

Craft felt is available in a wide variety of both strong and muted colours. It is made from natural wool fibres, so works well in conjunction with other woollen fabrics. Because it is not woven, the cut-out shapes will not fray, making felt particularly suited to the intricate and detailed shapes used here. Machine stitching in contrasting colours secures the motifs in position while adding a decorative touch.

Deer hart

You will need

Fringed tartan woollen scarf
Felt as follows:
    20cm (8in) square coral
    13 x 15cm (5 x 6in) olive green
    Scraps of black, white and lilac
Red heart-shaped button
80 white shirt buttons, 7mm (¼in)
    diameter
14 interestingly shaped wooden buttons
3 self-cover buttons, 2.5cm (1in)
    diameter
Scraps of red tartan fabric, to cover
    buttons
Red, black and white sewing threads
Green tweed-effect knitting yarn
Large-eyed needle
Fine-point indelible felt-tipped pen

To work the appliqué

1 Enlarge the deer and hart outlines given on page 63 to 156% on a photocopier and cut out. Trace off the heart outline and make a separate paper template for this.
2 Turn over the hart pattern and pin it to the coral felt. Draw lightly around the outside and the space between body and legs, using an indelible felt-tipped pen. Remove the template and cut out around the ink line using sharp scissors. Repeat for the deer template, using olive green felt. Cut out the heart from lilac felt. Felt is difficult to mark, so transferring the outlines of the templates in this way means that the ink line will not show on the right side. Cut out 3 small circles for the eyes from both black and white felt.

3 Pin the hart motif centrally at one end of the scarf 4cm (1½ in) from the fringe, so that it is facing towards the right. Tack in place, then machine stitch down using red sewing thread. Use a straight stitch and keep the stitching line about 3mm (⅛ in) in from the edge of the felt. Tack the lilac heart motif on to the hart's body and machine stitch down using red sewing thread. Sew the deer motif centrally on to the other end of the scarf 10cm (4in) from the fringe using red sewing thread, and attach a red heart-shaped button to its back. Stitch on the eyes for both animals by hand, placing the smaller black felt circles over the white circles.

To finish

1 The antlers for both deer and hart are made from tiny shirt buttons. Follow the lines on the template as a guide to placing, and stitch them on using white sewing thread.
2 Stitch 12 wooden buttons randomly around the hart, using tufts of green tweed-effect knitting yarn. Thread a large-eyed needle with a length of wool and sew the first button firmly in place. Leave the 2 loose ends at the front, knot securely and trim. Repeat for the other 11 buttons.
3 Following the manufacturer's instructions, cover 3 self-cover buttons with red tartan fabric. Use these and 2 more wooden buttons to decorate the opposite end of the scarf below the deer, stitching them on using tufts of yarn as before.

Dog wood

You will need

Fringed purple woollen scarf
Felt as follows:
  18 x 25cm (7 x 10in) lime green
  13 x 20cm (5 x 8in) orange
  13 x 20cm (5 x 8in) bright pink
  13cm (5in) square ochre
  Scraps of purple, dark green and rust
10mm (⅜in) shirt buttons:
  10 blue
  15 red
  3 yellow
Dark orange, red, dark blue and yellow
  sewing threads
Fine-point indelible felt-tipped pen

To work the appliqué

1 Enlarge the tree and dog outlines below and opposite to 156% on a photocopier, and cut out. Reversing the templates as for the Deer Hart scarf, draw lightly around the outlines using an indelible felt-tipped pen and cut out felt shapes as follows: a lime-green tree, an orange right-facing dog, a bright pink left-facing dog and an ochre left-facing half-dog. Also cut out 4 purple, 3 lime green, 3 rust and 10 dark green leaves.

2 Pin and tack the orange dog and the tree to one end of the scarf, and the bright pink and ochre dogs to the other end, 4cm (1½in) from the fringe (fig 1). Thread your machine with dark orange sewing thread and sew down the dogs with straight stitch, 3mm (⅛in) in from the edge of the felt. Stitch the tree in place with red sewing thread.

3 The dogs are decorated with buttons and felt leaves. The leaves are machine stitched on lengthways using yellow sewing thread. For the buttons, use contrasting or matching thread as required. Using the templates and photograph as a guide, stitch 4 purple leaves and 4 blue buttons on to the orange dog, and 3 lime green leaves and 3 yellow buttons on to the pink dog. Scatter the remaining 6 blue buttons across the ochre dog's body.

4 Machine stitch 10 dark green leaves around the tree and 3 rust-coloured leaves at the base of the trunk. Using a double length of red sewing thread, stitch the red buttons firmly on to the branches. Leave the ends of the thread at the front and trim to 2.5cm (1in).

fig 1

cut here for half-dog

dog for dog wood scarf

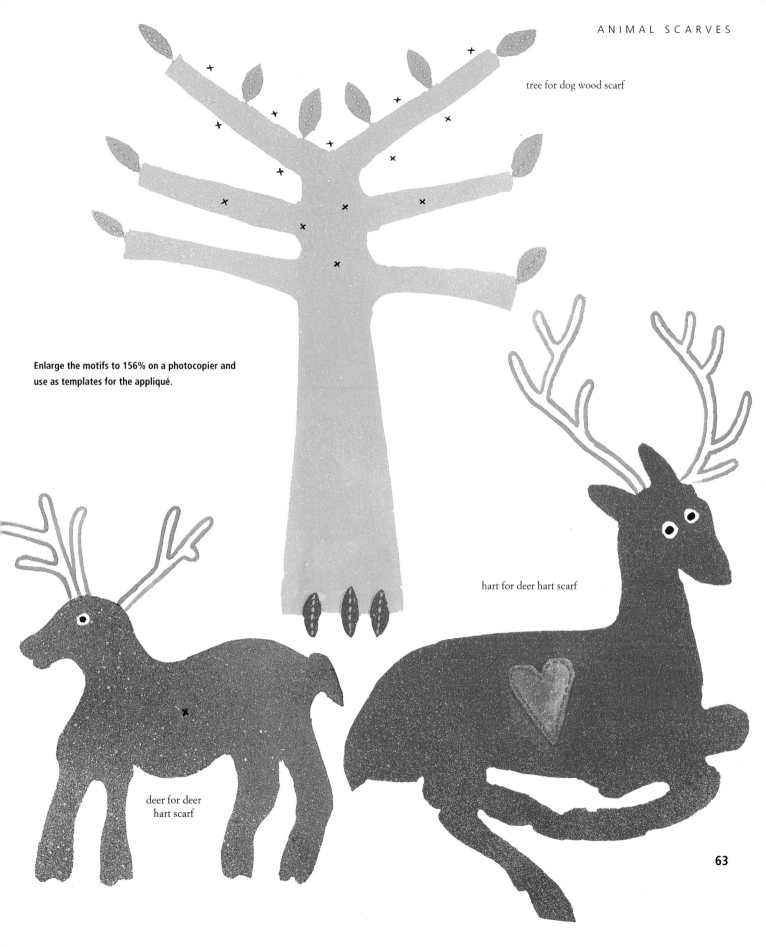

tree for dog wood scarf

Enlarge the motifs to 156% on a photocopier and
use as templates for the appliqué.

hart for deer hart scarf

deer for deer
hart scarf

Printed & patterned fabrics

Plain cottons and silks have been decorated using various printing techniques for many hundreds of years, to produce a wide array of patterned fabrics for clothing and interiors. The simplest hand-block methods have developed into the sophisticated screen- and roller-printing processes of today and a wealth of modern and traditional fabrics is now widely available.

Printed fabrics are a great source of inspiration for creating new appliqué designs. Individual motifs can be cut out from a patterned fabric; brightly coloured patterns can be used together with woven stripes, tweeds and ginghams to create a variety of new designs. The projects in this chapter show some of the ways in which fabrics can be combined.

broderie perse throw

A varied selection of upholstery offcuts and fabric samples in contrasting textures has been gathered together to make this broderie perse throw. The lush floral arrangement blends multicoloured motifs cut from glazed chintzes and union cloth with simple leaf shapes from co-ordinating plain fabrics. The white linen background gives a crispness to the design, which is highlighted by using embroidery stitches both to hold down the shapes and add detail. The piece is interlined to give it extra weight, and is backed using toning blue cotton fabric with a matching border of French knots.

You will need
For a finished throw 88cm (35in) square:
0.9m (1yd) heavy white linen fabric, 90cm (36in) wide
0.9m (1yd) blue cotton or linen fabric, 90cm (36in) wide, for backing
0.9m (1yd) calico, 90cm (36in) wide, for interlining
Assorted floral furnishing fabrics in various weights
20 x 30cm (8 x 12in) each red, blue and lime green cotton fabrics
20cm (8in) square emerald cotton fabric
Toning and contrasting pearl cottons
Matching and contrasting sewing threads

To prepare the appliqué
1 Sort through the furnishing fabrics, selecting the most interesting flower motifs in a range of sizes. Look for a variety of colours and shapes, making sure that some are complete with stems. Cut out about 20 assorted flowers, leaving a 6mm (¼in) seam allowance all round. Clip the curves and points, then fold back the turnings to the wrong side and tack down (fig 1).
2 Cut out at least 10 different printed leaves from the remaining furnishing fabrics, leaving a 6mm (¼in) seam allowance around each. Enlarge the template shapes for the leaves on page 69 to 150% on a photocopier. Using these as a guide, cut out about 35 plain-coloured leaves, in various sizes, from the 4 different-coloured plain cotton fabrics. Remember to add the seam allowance to each shape. Clip the curves and points and tack down the turnings.
3 Enlarge the template for the chrysanthemum-shaped flower on page

69 to 150% as before, and use as a guide to cut out a flower from plain blue cotton fabric, leaving a 6mm (¼in) seam allowance all round. Clip the curves and points and tack down the turnings.
4 Extra definition can be given to some of the motifs by mounting them on plain-coloured flower shapes. Select some cut-out and neatened printed flowers with strong outlines and draw around them on to the remaining red and green cotton fabric using a dressmaker's pen or chalk marking pencil. Cut out, leaving a margin of at least 2cm (¾in) all round. Clip the curves and points, turn under 6mm (¼in) and tack. Pin, then tack the printed flowers centrally on top of the plain ones (fig 2).
5 Enlarge the stylized butterfly template given on page 69 to 150% as before, and use as a guide to cut out one shape from a piece of suitably patterned furnishing fabric, leaving a 6mm (¼in) seam allowance all round.

To assemble the design
1 Press the white linen background fabric and check that the edges are squared up. Lay it out flat on your work surface and begin by placing the largest flowers in position. Create a visual focus by concentrating the motifs towards one corner, then scattering the rest across the square.
2 Place the leaves and the butterfly between the flowers, overlapping some and leaving space around others. Vary the density of the groupings to give balance to the design, and move the various motifs about until you are happy with the overall arrangement. Pin, then tack the motifs in their final positions.

fig 1

fig 2

fig 3

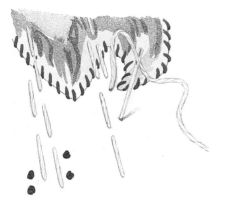

fig 4

fig 5

To embroider the motifs

1 Sew down each flower using a contrasting or toning shade of pearl cotton. Use overstitch or blanket stitch around the outer edges, then add further decoration with a selection of stitches in the same or another colour. Use French knots, stem stitch, satin stitch and straight stitch to highlight details such as petal outlines or the centres of the flowers. Embroider stamens from some of the flowers so that they extend on to the backing fabric, using straight stitch and French knots (fig 3).

2 Sew down the butterfly with an invisible slip stitch, using matching sewing thread. Embroider the details, using pearl cotton in colours to tone with the printed fabric. Work the body and wing markings in satin stitch. Add more details to the wings with French knots, circled by running stitch. Indicate the antennae with straight lines of running stitch, finished off with French knots (fig 4).

3 Stitch down the printed leaves in the same way as for the flowers, picking out

some of the printed lines with embroidery. Stitch down the plain leaves using matching or contrasting pearl cotton threads, and indicate the veins with feather, straight, stem or running stitches (fig 5).

4 Remove all the tacking threads and then press the appliqué from the right side, using a pressing cloth.

To make up

1 Press the blue cotton or linen backing fabric and the calico interlining. Place the appliqué right side up on your work surface. Position the interlining and then the backing fabric on top, lining up all the edges. Pin through all 3 layers.

2 Machine stitch around all 4 sides with a seam allowance of 12mm (½ in), leaving a 25cm (10in) gap at one side. Remove the pins and clip the corners.

3 Turn the throw right side out through the gap, and slip stitch the open sides together by hand. Press lightly from the reverse (blue) side.

4 Finish off by working a decorative line of French knots 6mm (¼ in) from the edge, using blue pearl cotton. Sew through the top layer of fabric only, working the stitches approximately 12mm (½ in) apart.

Enlarge the motifs to 150% on a photocopier and use as templates for the appliqué. Add a 6mm (1/4in) seam allowance when cutting out the fabric.

69

sporting cushions

These eclectic cushions use the new technique of image transfer, but would not have looked out of place in the study of an Edwardian country gentleman. Old black-and-white prints of sporting pursuits acquired from an antiquarian bookseller have been applied to cream cloth and combined with a mixture of fabrics – bright and muted tweeds, tartans and woven stripes. The final idiosyncratic detail comes from the accessories: blazer buttons, braids and golf tees.

Golf cushion

You will need

For a cushion 35cm (14in) square:
38cm (15in) square dark tartan fabric, for cushion front
38cm (15in) square matching tartan fabric, for cushion back
Brightly coloured tweed and tartan woollen fabric scraps
13 x 17cm (5 x 6¾ in) cream cotton fabric
Black sewing thread
Tweed effect double knitting yarn
12 wooden golf tees in assorted colours
Drill with fine bit
4 buttons, with golfing logo if possible
Illustration of golfer
Cream paper
Image transfer fluid (available from good haberdashers and art shops)
35cm (14in) square cushion pad

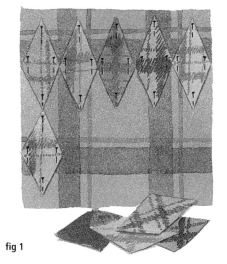

fig 1

To make the cushion front

1 Make a diamond template to the dimensions given on page 71 and cut out. Use the template as a guide to cut out 10 diamonds from brightly coloured tweed and tartan fabric scraps. Cut them so that they lie along the grain of the fabric, with stripes running from top to bottom. Pin and tack the diamonds in 2 rows of 5 on to the square of dark tartan fabric (fig 1).

2 Set your sewing machine to a wide zigzag and stitch around the edges of the diamond shapes so that the raw edges are covered.

3 Lay lengths of tweed effect double knitting yarn across the diamond shapes to form an Argyle pattern. The yarn should be parallel to the edges of the diamonds and cross in the centre of each shape. Pin, then stitch in place with a wide machine zigzag worked right over the yarn to hold it down (fig 2). Press the cushion front well.

4 Photocopy the golfing image that you have selected on to cream paper, enlarging or reducing it as necessary so that it fits on to the cream cotton fabric. Following the manufacturer's instructions, use image transfer fluid to

fig 2

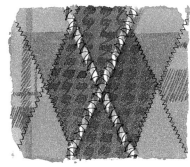

Enlarge this diamond template to 158mm (6¼in) high by 77mm (3in) wide.

transfer the picture centrally on to the cream fabric.

5 Place the golfer on the left-hand side of the cushion front and pin around the outside edge. Border the image with a double length of double knitting yarn to disguise the edge, then sew down with a wide zigzag as before.

To make up

1 With right sides together, pin the cushion back to the matching tartan fabric for the front. Sew around 3 sides with a seam allowance of 12mm (½in), leaving the bottom edge open. Clip the corners and turn the cover right side out. Use the pointed end of your embroidery scissors to ease the corners into shape and insert the cushion pad. Slip stitch the fourth side together. Sew a button to each corner of the cushion front.

2 To finish, use a drill with a fine bit to make a small hole approximately 8mm (⅜in) from the end of each of the golfing tees and sew 3 tees loosely on to each point of the cushion to form a 'tassel'.

71

Cricket cushion

fig 1

fig 2

You will need

For a cushion 33 x 44cm (13 x 17in):
35 x 45cm (14 x 18in) cream cotton
 fabric, for cushion front
35 x 45cm (14 x 18in) sea green moiré,
 for cushion back
4 differently patterned striped ties
1.5m (60in) striped braid, 2.5cm (1in)
 wide
1m (40in) striped braid, 1.5cm (½in) wide
Matching sewing threads
4 gold blazer buttons
Illustration of cricketer
Cream paper
Image transfer fluid (available from good
 haberdashers and art shops)
33 x 44cm (13 x 17in) cushion pad

To make the cushion front

1 Photocopy your image on to cream
paper, enlarging or reducing it to fit
within a rectangle measuring 16 x 19cm
(6¼ x 7½in). Use image transfer fluid to
transfer the image on to the cream
fabric, following the manufacturer's
instructions.

2 Cut 2 20cm (8in) lengths from each of
the striped braids. Pin, then sew a
narrow strip and a wide strip on either
side of the image.

3 Arrange the 4 ties to form a frame
around the centre panel. The wide points
should all overlap in the same direction.
Pin them in place and trim off the ends
(fig 1). Machine sew them down with
straight stitch, keeping the needle close
to the edges of the striped fabric.

To make the corner tabs

The 4 corners are all trimmed in the
same way. For each, cut 2 12cm (5in)
lengths from wide braid and one from
narrow braid. Fold the lengths in half
and pin to the right side of the corner, so
that the 2 wider loops lie along the
corners and the narrower loop points
towards the centre of the cushion. Tack
in place around the outer edge (fig 2).

To make up

1 With right sides together, pin the
cushion back to the front. Sew around
3 sides with a seam allowance of 12mm
(½in), leaving the bottom edge open.
Clip the corners and turn the cover right
side out. With the pointed end of your
embroidery scissors, ease the corners
into shape and insert the cushion pad.
Slip stitch the fourth side together.
2 Finish off by sewing a gold button to
each corner of the cushion front.

Fishing cushion

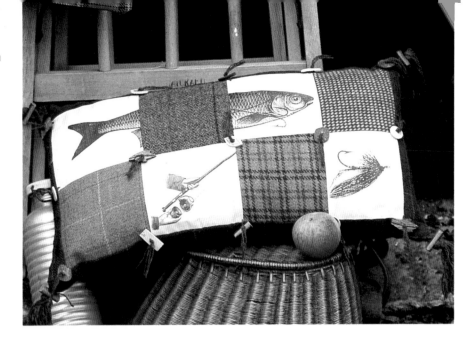

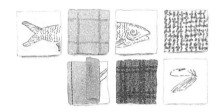

fig 1

fig 2

You will need

For a cushion 33 x 58cm (13 x 23in):
55 x 76cm (21½ x 30) brown tweed
15cm (6in) squares 4 more tweed fabrics
30cm (12in) square cream cotton fabric
15 wooden or coconut-shell buttons
Matching sewing threads
4 wooden toggle buttons
Tweed-effect brown 2-ply knitting yarn
Illustrations of angling subjects
Cream paper
Image transfer fluid (available from good
    haberdashers and art shops)
33 x 58cm (13 x 23in) cushion pad

To make the cushion front

1 Photocopy the angling images you
have selected on to cream paper,
reducing or enlarging so that each will fit
within a 15cm (6in) square. Cut the
cream fabric into 4 15cm (6in) squares
and, using image transfer fluid and
following the manufacturer's
instructions, transfer one picture on to
each square. A long shape can be
divided across 2 of the squares.
2 Alternate the 4 tweed and 4 picture
squares to make a checkerboard
rectangle of 2 by 4. Stitch them together
in 2 strips of 4, leaving a seam allowance
of 12mm (½in) (fig 1). Join the strips
lengthways, matching the seams. Press

the seams open: this must be done from
the back using a pressing cloth, so that
the heat does not damage the images.
3 Cut out a rectangle of brown tweed
fabric 36 x 61cm (14 x 24in) for the
cushion back. From the remaining fabric,
cut 2 strips 6.5 x 61 (2½ x 24in) and 2
strips 6.5 x 28cm (2½ x 11in) to form a
border for the patchwork panel. Sew the
2 short lengths along the short ends of
the panel, then sew the 2 long lengths
along the long sides. Press the seams
open from the back as before.
4 Use double lengths of tweed-effect
yarn to stitch the buttons at the corners
of each square. Knot the ends and trim
to 6cm (2½in) to form a tuft.

To make up

1 With right sides facing, pin the cushion
back to the front around one short and
2 long sides. Stitch, leaving a seam
allowance of 12mm (½in). Clip the
corners and turn right side out. With the
points of your embroidery scissors, ease
the corners into shape and Insert the
cushion pad. Slip stitch the fourth side.
2 To make a tassel for each corner,
thread several strands of tweed-effect
yarn through the holes in a toggle
button. Tie in a knot and trim to 6cm
(2½in). Sew firmly in place (fig 2).

73

floral tablecloth

Printed and woven fabrics are often used in a highly extravagant fashion, combining every variation of texture, pattern and colour. This unmistakably contemporary tablecloth demonstrates how a much simpler approach can be equally dramatic, bringing appliqué right up to date for a modern interior.

The success of such a minimalist treatment depends on a refined balance of form and stitch, along with the careful selection of fabrics. The counterchange of the yellow and white linen background of the cloth is balanced by the precise placing of the stylized appliqué and embroidered flowers.

You will need

For a finished tablecloth about 147cm (58in) square:

0.8m (⅞yd) white linen fabric, 150cm (60in) wide

76cm (30in) square yellow linen fabric

76cm (30in) square yellow-and-white check cotton fabric

30 x 50cm (12 x 20in) cotton fabric in 2 shades of green

Scraps of plain, check and floral fabrics, including woven numbers and sprig prints

Matching and contrasting sewing threads

Assorted embroidery threads

To make the cloth

1 Cut the white linen fabric into 2 76cm (30in) squares. Pin, then machine stitch one of the pieces along one edge of the square of yellow linen fabric, with a seam allowance of 12mm (½in). Press the seam open. Fold under the surplus fabric along either side of the seam and press flat. Machine stitch down using matching sewing thread (fig 1). Join the second square of white linen to the square of yellow-and-white check cotton fabric in the same way.

2 Join the 2 rectangles together, so that the white squares are diagonally opposite. Neaten the seam as before, then finish the outside edge with a narrow double hem, machine stitched using a contrasting thread.

To prepare the appliqué and assemble the design

1 Cut 12 tapering strips from the 2 shades of green cotton fabric. These should vary in size, from 2–4cm (¾–1½in) wide and from 23–45cm (9–18in) long. Neaten the edges by pressing under an allowance of 6mm (¼in) all round.

2 Place the strips on the cloth, adjusting their positions to give a balanced overall composition. When you are satisfied with the arrangement, pin, then machine stitch down the strips using matching green sewing threads.

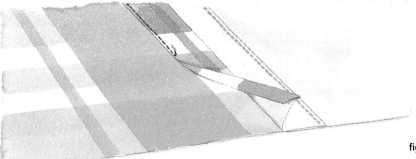

fig 1

fig 2

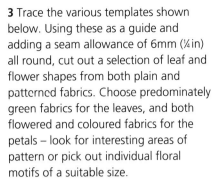

3 Trace the various templates shown below. Using these as a guide and adding a seam allowance of 6mm (¼ in) all round, cut out a selection of leaf and flower shapes from both plain and patterned fabrics. Choose predominately green fabrics for the leaves, and both flowered and coloured fabrics for the petals – look for interesting areas of pattern or pick out individual floral motifs of a suitable size.

4 Clip the curves of the motifs and press under the edges. Take some time in arranging the motifs on the cloth until you are happy with the design, then pin them to the cloth and machine stitch down around the edges using matching sewing threads

To embroider the motifs and background
1 Add contrasting coloured detail to the flowers and stems, either by hand with lines of running or straight stitch using embroidery thread (fig 2), or by machine with the controls set to the longest straight stitch. Using bright red thread, stitch tulip-shaped petals at the top of one of the stems, filling them with lines of backstitch or straight machine stitching. Using contrasting colours of sewing thread, work long lines of machine straight stitch across the width of the cloth.

2 Hand embroider decorative circles and random patterns of backstitch, running stitch, stem stitch and French knots over the surface of the cloth (fig 3).

These templates are shown actual size. Add a 6mm (¼in) seam allowance all around when cutting out the fabric.

fig 3

Lace, ribbons & organza

Lace has always been the ultimate luxury fabric. Handmade lace cuffs and collars were once worn as status symbols by both men and women of fashion and lace has long been favoured by dressmakers to add the final touch to a special outfit. Well-chosen trimmings can also give a decorative, opulent finish to other needlecrafts, particularly appliqué.

Trimmings can be sewn to contrasting, functional fabrics, such as unbleached calico, for a striking effect, or used together with net, silk organzas or cotton voile for more ethereal results. Lengths of ribbon or braid may be used to border a design, conceal a seam or even to create an extravagant fabric made up entirely of appliquéd bands of complementary colours and textures. With imagination, purely ornamental fabrics and trimmings can be combined to create some stunning and original effects.

using trimmings

Most people who enjoy sewing collect together a ragbag over time. Among the remnants of different fabrics, there may be scraps of more luxurious materials such as velvets and organzas. There is also likely to be an accumulation of various trimmings – ribbons, braids, cords and fringing, as well as offcuts of lace – and all of these can be incorporated into your appliqué projects. The Cactus Cushions on pages 88–93 are a wonderful example of how this can be done.

Ribbon

Ribbons have been used for many years both to hold together and to adorn garments and furnishing accessories. Decorative ribbon can be purchased in a wide variety of widths, textures and colours, ranging from translucent voiles, ribbed petersham and tartans, to printed striped, spotted or patterned satins.

• Ribbon can be used with restraint in an appliqué design to provide a contrasting strip of colour, or several ribbons can be interwoven to a give an interesting multicoloured effect.
• Lavish ribbons can be gathered into rosettes or tied into bows as extra embellishment to trim an item.

• The woven edges make ribbon simple to sew down with hand stitching or by machine, as there are no raw edges to turn under. However, the stitching on both edges must always run in the same direction, for example, from top to bottom, to prevent the ribbon becoming puckered and distorted.

Organza

Organza is a translucent fabric woven from silk, acetate or metallic threads which is usually chosen by dressmakers to create extravagant ball gowns and evening dresses, or by milliners for adorning hats. On a smaller scale, it can be used very successfully for appliqué, both as a delicate background fabric and for lustrous motifs.

• Organza can be sewn on to or inserted into opaque fabrics, but it is most effective when layered with net, voile or other sheer materials to exploit the play of light on the surface of the fabric. The Herb Bags on pages 82–85 show how subtle and unexpected colour effects can be achieved in this way.

• Shot organza is woven from a contrasting warp and weft, which gives it an iridescent appearance. It is possible to utilize this quality by cutting out square or rectangular shapes along the grain of the fabric and fringing the cut edges to show the different-coloured silk, gold or silver threads.

Lace Modern machine lace is available in many decorative forms. Edgings are produced in various widths and weights, and lace is also manufactured in fabric widths for dressmaking. It is usually white, but can be dyed to any colour for a more unconventional look. An antique beige tint can be given to new cotton lace by dipping it in cold tea or coffee.

Net-based laces, which are derived from traditional bobbin or needlepoint lace patterns, are often too fine to be used for any work which will need to withstand much wear, but thicker *guipure* lace, with its well-defined patterns, is ideal for appliqué. It can be used in two different ways – either applied on top of another fabric or inset into a background.

Applied lace

Choose a lace with a strong design and cut out individual motifs using sharp embroidery scissors. Some types will not fray, but in order to prevent any unravelling it may be necessary to coat the back of the lace with a fray-prevention liquid (see page 24). This will give the lace a slightly stiffer texture which is easier to handle.

• Arrange the motifs on the background fabric and pin in place. Large motifs should be tacked down, to prevent any wrinkles. Sew down with neat overstitches around the outside edges, using matching thread.

• Be careful not to pull the thread too tightly, especially when using a lightweight background fabric. A densely woven background, such as cotton or linen, will create a very different effect to a net or other sheer fabric.

Lace insertion

When lace is inset into a background, it becomes part of the fabric itself. If the lace is to be attached to a fine cloth, or you are working by hand on a small scale, the main fabric should be supported in an embroidery frame. For larger-scale work on heavier fabric, use a sewing machine to stitch the lace into position and to neaten the edges with satin stitch.

• To insert by hand, cut out a single lace motif. Pin, then tack it on to the background fabric. Stitch down neatly with blanket stitch or overstitch around the outside edges of the motif, using matching thread (fig 1).

Turn over and carefully cut away the fabric from within the shape (fig 2) – nail scissors with small curved blades are ideal for this.

• To insert by machine, draw a shape on to a piece of lace using a dressmaker's pen or cut out a motif, leaving a margin of 6mm (¼in) around the edge. Pin the lace on to the background and tack it down securely.

Stitch over the drawn outline, then trim away the surplus lace from the front, and the background fabric from behind, as above. Work a line of closely spaced machine satin stitch to conceal and strengthen the raw edges.

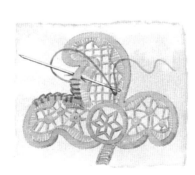

fig 1

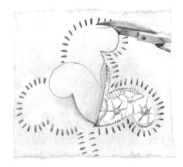

fig 2

herb bags

The translucent qualities of metallic organzas are exploited to the full to make these opulent herb bags. The sumptuous texture of the crushed velvet hearts contrasts with the delicacy of the sheer silk organzas, and the multi-layered fabrics create a rich density of colour. Lustrous beads, gold cords and tassels are added as luxurious details.

The bags are very simple to put together and can be made in any size or combination of colours. They can be filled with dried flowers or herbs, as here, so that the colours of the leaves and petals show through the sheer fabrics, or used as presentation bags for a special Christmas or birthday gift.

Rose bag

fig 1

You will need

36 x 45cm (14 x 18in) pale gold crystal organza
16 x 45cm (6¼ x 18in) silver crystal organza
Scraps of purple, pink and turquoise shot-silk organzas
Scraps of gold and bronze metallic organzas
Matching sewing threads
About 200 tiny metallic beads in various bright colours
Fine crewel needle (size 10 or 11)
Rose pot-pourri to fill

To work the appliqué and beading

1 Cut out 9 4cm (1½in) squares from the different shot-silk organzas, and fringe the edges by carefully pulling out a few threads along each side. Cut out a 12cm (5in) square of silver crystal organza and fringe the edges. Arrange the small squares on it in 3 rows of 3, alternating the colours.
2 Using the 3 smallest templates shown below as a guide, cut out 9 different-sized hearts from metallic organzas and pin each one to a contrasting square.
3 The appliqué is held on by the beading. Using a double length of matching sewing thread and the fine needle, stitch the metallic beads 3mm (⅛in) inside the edge of the hearts (fig 1).

To make up

1 Hand sew the appliquéd panel to the centre front of the pale gold crystal organza rectangle 4cm (1½in) from the lower short edge, using matching thread. With the appliqué on the inside, join the side edges by hand or machine. Fold the bag in half so that the seam runs up the centre back, and join the bottom seam. Turn right side out.
2 Fold under the top 15cm (6in) of the bag fabric and run a gathering stitch through both layers, 9cm (3½in) from the top. Fill the bag with rose pot-pourri and draw up the gathering thread.
3 Cut out a 45 x 4cm (18 x 1½in) strip of organza and tie it around the top, with the bow facing towards the back.

These assorted heart motifs for the three herb bags are shown actual size.

Gold bag

You will need

25 x 30cm (10 x 12in) bronze Fortuny-pleat metallic fabric

Scrap of red velvet

Scraps of bronze and red shot metallic organzas

75cm (30in) gold cord

Matching sewing threads

Gold machine embroidery threads

Small piece of cardboard

Dried herbs to fill

To work the appliqué

1 Using the largest template shown on page 82 as a guide, cut out a heart from red velvet. Cut out a rectangle 9 x 10cm (3½ x 4in) from red shot metallic organza and a 6 x 7cm (2½ x 3in) rectangle from bronze. Fringe the edges of both by carefully pulling out a few threads along each side. Place the smaller rectangle on top of the larger, and then pin the velvet heart in the centre.

2 Sew the heart through both pieces of organza with tiny overstitches, leaving a small space at centre top. Slip one end of

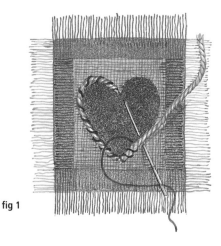

fig 1

the gold cord under the velvet at this point, then couch it around the edge of the heart using matching sewing thread (fig 1). Trim the end of the cord to 12mm (½in), tuck it under the velvet and overstitch the cut edge.

To make up

1 Sew the appliquéd panel to the centre front of the Fortuny-pleat metallic fabric, 5cm (2in) from the lower long edge. With the appliqué on the inside, join the two short edges by hand or machine, then fold in half so that the centre seam runs up the back and sew together the lower edge.

2 Unravel a few long threads from the top edge to make a narrow fringe. Turn right side out.

3 Make 2 tassels about 9cm (3½in) long, using gold machine embroidery thread. Knot the ends of the remaining gold cord and sew one tassel to each end, concealing the cut strands.

4 Fill the bag with dried herbs, then tie the cord in a bow around the top.

Lavender bag

You will need

43 x 45cm (17 x 18in) silver crystal organza

6 x 14cm (2½ x 5½in) gold metallic organza

Scraps of emerald and lilac velvet

Scraps of metallic organza in golds, greens and blues

Matching sewing threads

About 180 translucent 3mm (⅛in) glass beads

Fine crewel needle (size 10 or 11)

Metallic sewing thread

60cm (24in) gold cord

Dried lavender to fill

To work the appliqué

1 Trace the 4 smaller heart templates shown on page 82 on to paper. Selecting from these, draw 3 hearts on to the reverse of each of the emerald and lilac velvet fabrics and cut out.

2 Cut out a rectangle 6 x 14cm

(2½ x 5½in) from gold metallic organza, and a rectangle 5 x 13cm (2 x 5in) from silver crystal organza. Cut out 3 4cm (1½in) squares and 3 3cm (1¼in) squares from the various scraps of organza. Fringe the edges of all the pieces by carefully pulling out a few threads along each side.

3 Place the smaller organza rectangle on top of the larger one, then arrange the 3 larger organza squares in a row. Set the smaller squares on to them at an angle, then pin a velvet heart on to each square. Sew the hearts in place with small overstitches, using matching sewing threads. Make sure that you stitch through all the layers of organza.

4 Cut out a rectangle 38 x 45 (15 x 18in) from silver crystal organza to make the main bag and fringe one of the short sides to form the lower edge. Pin the appliquéd organza panel to the centre front, 5cm (2in) from the bottom.

To sew on the beads

1 The panel is held on by the beading. Using a double length of matching sewing thread and the fine needle, stitch glass beads as close as possible to the edge of the velvet hearts, spacing them evenly.

2 Pin the remaining 3 hearts on to the main bag, scattering them above the appliquéd panel. Sew them down with tiny overstitches using matching sewing thread, then edge with a line of beading as above.

To make up the bag

1 With the appliqué on the inside, join the side edges by hand or machine. Turn right side out and then fold so that the seam runs up the centre back. Close the lower edge of the bag with a line of running stitch using matching metallic sewing thread and the fine needle, threading on a glass bead as you work each few stitches (fig 1).

2 Make a knot at each end of the gold cord and unravel the threads to create a tassel effect. Fold under the top 15cm (6in) of the bag fabric and run a gathering stitch through both layers, 9cm (3½in) from the top. Fill the bag with dried lavender, and draw up the gathering thread. Secure the ends tightly, then finish off by tying the gold cord in a bow.

fig 1

85

ribbon bolster

The attractive striped pattern on this bolster cushion is formed by stitching bands of ribbon on to a taffeta background. Its strong visual impact is achieved by using a varied assortment of fabric textures, but limiting the colour scheme to a narrow range. Some ribbons are overlapped to give extra density to the colour, while in other places parts of the tartan background show through. The embroidery stitches which hold the ribbons in place are reminiscent of those used to decorate Victorian 'crazy patchwork'.

You will need

For a bolster 50cm (20in) long:

110cm (43in) lengths of at least 15 ribbons in different widths, textures and colours

54 x 64cm (21 x 25in) dark striped or tartan taffeta fabric, stripes running parallel to shorter edges

Toning and contrasting pearl cottons

Matching sewing threads

Strong thread, such as buttonhole thread, for gathering

50cm (20in) bolster cushion pad, 50cm (20in) circumference

2 furnishing tassels (optional)

To work the appliqué

1 Cut the lengths of ribbon in half and place them on the taffeta fabric so that they lie parallel to the shorter edges. Use the stripes of the fabric as a guide to keeping the ribbons straight, and leave 12mm (½in) uncovered at each short edge. Butt up the edges of most of the ribbons, but leave narrow gaps between others so that the taffeta shows. Overlap some of the plain colours with the sheer ribbons. Adjust them until you have a good balance of colour and texture.

2 Pin, then tack down the ribbons carefully along both edges. Work each line of tacking in the same direction to prevent puckering (fig 1).

3 Secure the ribbons with lines of embroidery worked in contrasting or toning pearl cottons. Use simple stitches including herringbone, feather, running and whipped running stitch, but vary the width, length and spacing to give extra interest to the surface. When all the ribbons have been sewn down, unpick the tacking.

To make up

1 With right sides facing, pin together the long edges of the appliquéd taffeta, ensuring that the cut ends of the ribbons match. Machine stitch together, leaving a seam allowance of 12mm (½in), then turn the cover right side out.

2 Place the cover over the bolster: it should fit tightly. Turn under the taffeta at each short edge and, using a double length of strong thread, stitch with a line of evenly spaced running stitches, about 12mm (½in) long. Pull up this thread tightly so that the ends of the bolster are covered. Make sure that the gathers are evenly spaced, then finish off with a few overstitches to secure.

3 Conceal the gathered ends with a trimming such as tassels or ribbon bows.

fig 1

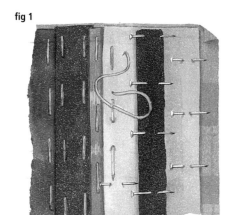

cactus cushions

An extravagant, unrestrained use of colour within a carefully chosen palette characterizes these large and exuberant cushions. The cotton lace belies its delicate appearance and has been combined with unexpected fabrics including towelling, over-dyed gingham, velvet and organza. Furnishing braids, bullion and pompon fringing, beads and ribbons in matching and clashing shades add texture and pattern to both the fronts and backs of the cushion covers. This is a project that is open to a very individual interpretation – search through your ragbag to find an assortment of interesting and unusual fabrics and indulge in a vibrant riot of colour.

Rectangular cushion

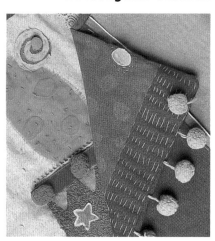

You will need

For a cushion 40 x 60cm (16 x 24in):
For the front panel and appliqué:
Remnants and scraps of fabric in assorted patterns, textures and colours
Assorted thick cotton lace, pompon fringing, bullion fringing, cord, ribbon and ricrac braid
Ribbon rose
Matching sewing thread
Contrasting pearl, stranded and soft embroidery cottons
Fabric glue
For the back:
20 x 63.5cm (8 x 25in) cotton fabric
32 x 63.5cm (12½ x 25in) contrasting cotton fabric
63.5cm (25in) braid
Contrasting stranded cotton
3 self-cover buttons, 20mm (¾in) diameter
63.5cm (25in) pompon fringing
40 x 60cm (16 x 24in) cushion pad

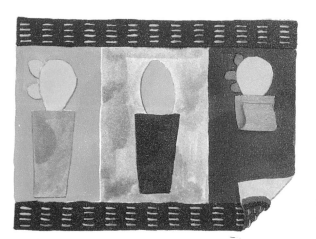

fig 1

To make the front panel

1 Cut out 3 rectangles from contrasting bright cotton fabrics: 2 24 x 36cm (9½ x 14in) and one 20 x 36cm (8 x 14in). Join them together with a seam allowance of 12mm (½in), to make a rectangle measuring 36 x 63.5cm (14 x 25in). Press seams open.
2 Cut out 2 63.5cm (25in) strips, each 6cm (2½in) wide, in a fourth colour, and sew to each long side of the main fabric with a 12mm (½in) seam allowance. Press the seams open. Decorate the strips with parallel lines of large running stitch, worked in a contrasting embroidery thread.

To work the appliqué

1 Enlarge the 3 outlines on page 92 to 156% and then to 125% on a photocopier and trace off the main elements of each template. Using these as a guide, cut out the cacti and their pots from an assortment of fabrics. Arrange the pieces on the background using fig 1 and the photograph opposite as a guide. Stick down using fabric glue.
2 Cut out the stars, circles and stripes that trim the pots, and the small dots and circles that decorate the cacti, and glue in place. Add further embellishment to the appliqué with pompons cut from lengths of fringing, ribbons, bullion fringing and lace, ricrac braid and a ribbon rose.
3 Embroider the details using a variety of embroidery threads in bright colours: straight stitch for the spikes around the edges of the cacti, running-stitch lines to hold down the ricrac braid and couching to secure coloured cord.

fig 2

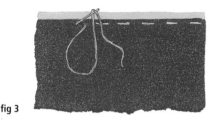

fig 3

fig 4

To make the cushion back

1 Cut out 2 rectangles, one 20 x 63.5cm (8in x 25in) and one 32 x 63.5cm (12½ x 25in), from contrasting cotton fabrics. Also cut out a 63.5cm (25in) strip, 6cm (2½in) wide, from fabric to match the narrower piece.

2 Neaten one long edge of the larger rectangle. Turn under a 5cm (2in) hem.

3 Trim one long edge of the narrower rectangle with braid, by stitching it in between the main fabric and the strip, with the right side of the braid facing the right side of the main fabric (fig 2). Turn back the strip and press. Topstitch with a line of running stitch, using stranded cotton in a bright colour (fig 3).

4 Make 3 evenly spaced buttonholes on the braid-trimmed piece. For each one,

fig 5

cut out a 4cm (1½in) square of contrasting fabric and draw an opening 2.5cm x 5mm (1 x ¼in) on the centre. Tack the square to the right side of the fabric and sew around the outline by hand or machine. Slit the fabric inside the stitching, cutting carefully into the corners (fig 4), and push the remaining fabric to the wrong side. Press, then topstitch the opening with stranded cotton in a bright colour (fig 5). Neaten the cut edges of the fabric at the back.

To make up

1 Pin pompon fringing along the bottom edge of the appliquéd front of the cushion, with the pompons facing inwards. With right sides together, pin the trimmed back piece along this edge, then pin the second back piece in place so that it overlaps the first. Sew all around the outside, with a seam allowance of 12mm (½in). Turn the cushion cover right side out.

2 Following the manufacturer's instructions, cover 3 self-cover buttons with different-coloured fabrics and sew in place on the back of the cushion. Insert the cushion pad into the cover.

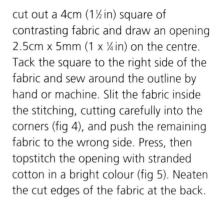

Square cushion

You will need

For a cushion 60cm (24in) square:
For the front panel and appliqué:
Remnants and scraps of fabric in assorted patterns, textures and colours
3 30 x 38cm (12 x 15in) pieces different-coloured cotton fabrics, for the scallops
Assorted cords, ribbons, pompons, fringing, beads, ricrac braid and felt
Matching sewing thread
Contrasting pearl, stranded and soft embroidery cottons
Fabric glue
For the back:
45 x 63.5cm (18 x 25in) cotton fabric
13 x 63.5cm (5 x 25in) matching cotton fabric

30 x 63.5cm (12 x 25in) contrasting cotton fabric
Self-cover buttons:
  3 3cm (1¼in) diameter
  2 2cm (¾in) diameter
Felt scraps
Beads and/or embroidery threads as above
5 clear press-fasteners
60cm (24in) square cushion pad

To join the front cover

Cut out 3 rectangles from contrasting cotton fabrics, one 28cm x 63.5cm (11 x 25in), one 37 x 39cm (14½ x 15½in) and one 27 x 37cm (10½ x 14½in). Join them together to make a 63.5cm (25in) square, using fabric glue and simple running and overstitches.

fig 1

To work the appliqué

1 Enlarge the templates on pages 92 and 93 to 156% and then to 125% on a photocopier and trace off a separate pattern for each. Cut out the cactus parts and the flowerpots and, using fig 1 and the photograph on page 89 as a guide, glue them on to the background.
2 Cut out the various stars that surround the smaller cactus, and the stars and circles that decorate the larger one and its pot, and glue them in place (fig 1). Sew beads, pompons and lengths of ribbon and ricrac braid on to and around the pots and cacti. Embroider lines of running and straight stitch to highlight the motifs and to indicate the spikes around the cacti, using various threads.

To make the scallops

Enlarge the scallop template on page 93 to 156% and then to 125% on a photocopier. You will need 16 scallops in assorted colours. For each scallop, cut 2 pieces of matching fabric, using the template as a guide. With right sides facing, stitch them together around the curved side, with a seam allowance of 6mm (¼ in). Clip the curves, turn right side out and press flat.

To prepare the cushion back

1 Neaten one long edge on the narrow strip of cotton fabric for the cushion back. To make a wavy edge on the larger rectangle for the cushion back, pin the narrow strip along one edge with right sides facing and matching cut edges.
2 On the strip, draw a regular wavy line with 5 equidistant points 6mm (¼ in) from the cut edge (fig 2) and machine

stitch along the line. Trim the 2 layers of fabric 6mm (¼ in) outside the wavy line. Clip the seam allowance and turn the fabric right side out. Press the wavy edge, then topstitch it with a line of large-scale running stitch using a contrasting embroidery thread. Neaten one long edge on the other back piece.

To make up

1 Lay the appliquéd piece right side up. Arrange 4 scallops pointing inwards along each of the 4 edges.
2 Place the wavy-edged backing piece face down on the appliquéd square, matching cut edges along the bottom and with the wavy edge towards the centre. Place the other backing piece face down along the other side, with the neatened edge towards the centre. Pin down, then sew around all 4 sides, 12mm (½ in) from the edge. Turn the cushion cover right side out.

To finish

1 Cover the 5 self-cover buttons with different-coloured fabrics, following the manufacturer's instructions. Enlarge the flower template on page 93 to 156% and then to 125% on a photocopier. Using the template as a guide, cut out 5 flower shapes from felt. Snip a tiny hole in the centre of each and fit it over the shank before attaching the back piece (fig 3). Embellish each button with French knots or beads.
2 Sew one button on to each point of the wavy edge. Sew a clear press-fastener under the tip of each point, lining up the 2 parts on both sides of the cover. Insert the cushion pad.

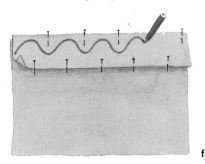

fig 2

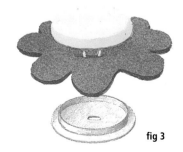

fig 3

91

cactus templates for rectangular cushion

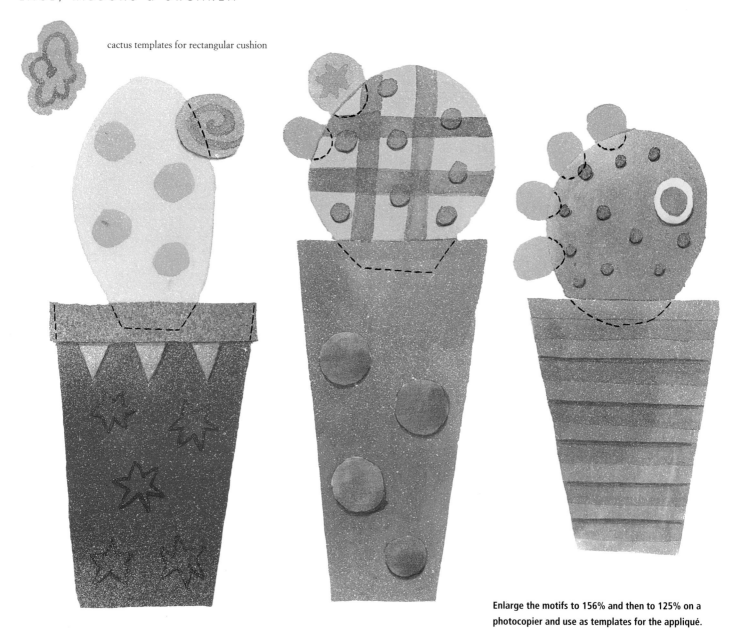

Enlarge the motifs to 156% and then to 125% on a photocopier and use as templates for the appliqué.

star templates for square cushion

template for the
floral buttons on
the square cushion

cactus templates for the square cushion

scallop template for square cushion

93

lace blind

The formal lines of this classic roller blind are softened by the light filtering through the appliquéd lace cut-outs. The blind provides a dramatic focus to a room, and the muted tones of unbleached calico and cotton lace will blend with any colour scheme – old lace may be too fragile to withstand everyday use, but new lace can be dipped in tea to give it an antique appearance. The main central motif contains a single initial to add a personal touch, but this can be replaced by a house or apartment number if the blind is to hang at a front window. An alphabet and a set of numerals are given on pages 106–107.

Roller-blind kits, containing all the necessary fitments and instructions, are widely available in standard sizes which can be adapted easily to fit your own window. Finish off the lower edge with a wooden blind pull or a cream tassel.

You will need

Heavyweight unbleached calico, 10cm (4in) wider and 30cm (12in) longer than your window
63cm (25in) cotton lace, 12cm (5in) wide, or scraps of old lace and doilies
15 x 30cm (6 x 12in) cotton net, for main central motif
12cm (5in) square unbleached calico, for initial or number
Cream sewing thread
Roller-blind kit and spray-on fabric stiffener
Sticky tape

To mark out the design

1 Enlarge the template on page 96 to 156% and then to 112% on a photocopier. Make a second copy. Reverse one section of the design and join the 2 halves to make a symmetrical stencil. Cut out the various shapes carefully.
2 Fold the unbleached calico for the blind in half lengthways and press lightly to mark the centre line. Pin the stencil along this line, so that it lies 15cm (6in) from the bottom edge. Using the stencil as a guide, mark the design on to the fabric using a dressmaker's pen (fig 1).

To work the appliqué

1 Cut lengths of lace to fit over the various small outlined sections of the design, allowing a minimum overlap of 12mm (½in) all round. Pin, then tack them in place 6mm (¼in) outside the outline of each shape, making sure that the lace lies flat (fig 2). If the outline has become indistinct, draw over it again on to the lace. Using cream sewing thread, work straight machine stitch over the outline, stitching slowly to achieve smooth curves.
2 Trim back the surplus lace to within 3mm (⅛in) of the stitched line, using sharp embroidery scissors (fig 3). Turn over the fabric and carefully cut out the calico from within the shapes, to within 3mm (⅛in) of the stitching. Sew over the cut edges with a wide, medium-spaced zigzag stitch, to neaten and strengthen the seams.

fig 1

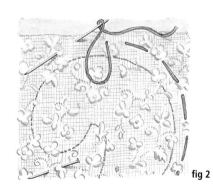

fig 2

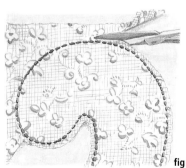

fig 3

3 Inset cotton net into the main central motif in the same way. Either decorate the central motif with small shapes cut from lace scraps, or with an appliquéd number or letter cut from unbleached calico. Tack, then hand sew or zigzag stitch in place.

4 Press well to remove the creases, using a pressing cloth to protect the lace.

To make up

Check that the edges of the calico are square; trim them if not, then spray with fabric stiffener. Follow the instructions supplied with the kit to make up the blind. Screw the fitments to the wall as instructed, and fix the roller in place.

Half the design for the Lace blind is shown here. Enlarge to 156% and then to 112% on a photocopier. Repeat to make a second copy. Reverse one half and join to the other along the centre line to make a symmetrical shape.

centre line

Patterns &
motifs

The following pages offer a range of additional design motifs which will complement the projects in the earlier chapters and provide inspiration for you to develop further your own ideas. They include templates for four more country-style floral patterns, variations on the natural imagery of leaves and snowflakes, more distinctive nursery appliqué shapes for children, and finally two versatile alphabets that can be used on any scale to personalize your work.

block motifs

See Baltimore Bride Cushion on page 20

These blocks are inspired by antique originals but have been adapted to incorporate the distinctive floral motif from the Baltimore bride cushion. Like the rose-filled basket, the cornucopia is a symbol of abundance, often used on wedding quilts, and this example overflows with fruits and flowers. A full-sized appliqué bed cover is a true labour of love, but these four traditional patterns could be used together to make a cot cover or wall hanging. To achieve smooth curves, the circle for the garland and the curved stalks should all be made from bias strips (see page 16). Enlarge or reduce the motifs on a photocopier as required.

pattern-cut snowflakes

See Snowflake Cushions on page 32

A huge variety of symmetrical patterns can be cut from folded paper. These can then form the starting point for creating intricate pattern-cut appliqué designs. To make a square shape, fold the paper diagonally in half, then into quarters, then into eighths and press the creases firmly in place. Trace one section of the motif on to the triangle of folded paper and cut out. For a six-sided motif, fold the paper in half. Mark angles of 60° and 120° from the centre and fold again along these lines to give six segments, then fold the paper again before transferring the snowflake outline on to the top layer. Enlarge or reduce the motifs as required on a photocopier.

leaf collection

See Leaf Table Linen on page 42

The morning glory, ivy and passion flower templates can be used singly or arranged to form sprays to match the other leaf designs. The beech and silver birch leaves illustrated here are both used on the bright cotton tablecloth, but all of these designs could be adapted to a more naturalistic colour scheme of summer greens or browns, yellows and russets. Try cutting out an assortment of leaves in different shapes and sizes and arranging them randomly so that they overlap to create a true autumnal feel. Enlarge the motifs to 136% on a photocopier.

ivy

beech

passion flower

silver birch

horse chestnut

morning glory

103

nursery images

See Alphabet Quilt on page 56

These motifs – which include winter mittens, a car, a shell and an ice cream – are intended as variations for the red-and-white alphabet play quilt, but could equally well decorate children's clothes, bedlinen, toy bags or playroom cushions and curtains. The original quilt is made up in a restrained two-colour combination, but try using a range of brightly coloured cottons or small-scale dress prints for a more lively effect. Enlarge or reduce the motifs as required on a photocopier.

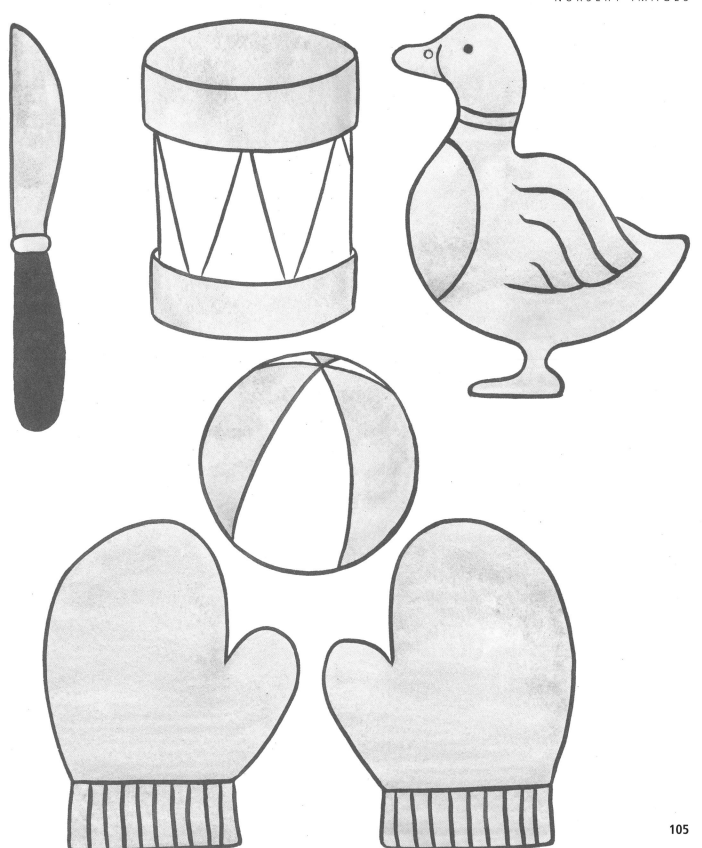

alphabets & numerals

Large or small single capital letters can be used to form monograms or sets of initials which add an individual finish to any appliqué project or gift, or you may choose them to build up words, names or short phrases. The plainer alphabet overleaf is used on the Alphabet quilt on page 56 and the more ornate period variation shown here is intended for the Lace blind on page 94, but either of them could be incorporated into other designs.

The two sets of numerals can also be adapted to many different purposes. To use as templates for the Lace blind, enlarge the letters or numerals shown here to 156%, then 156%, then 140% on a photocopier.

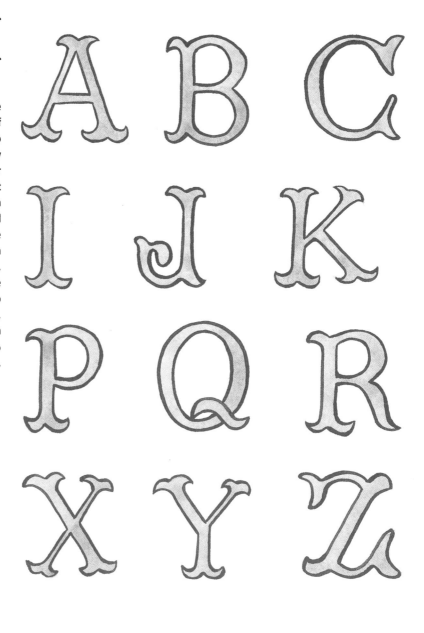

D E F G H
L M N O
S T U V W

6 7 8 9 0

A B C D E
L M N O P
V W X Y Z
a b c d e f
n o p q r s t
1 2 3 4 5 6

F G H I J K
Q R S T U

Enlarge the alphabets and numerals shown
here to 156% and then to 106% on a
photocopier and use as templates for the
Alphabet quilt on page 56.

g h i j k l m
U V W X Y Z

7 8 9 0

index

acknowledgments

The author would like to thank everybody who has been involved in creating this book, particularly the editorial and design team at Quadrille who made it all possible: Mary Evans, Jane O'Shea, Patsy North, Vanessa Courtier, Kate Simunek for the illustrations, Pia Tryde for the photographs , and especially Gabi Tubbs for her inspiration.

Special thanks to Christine Kingdom at C. M. Offray & Son Ltd and Carole Tompkins for their help, and to my family for their unfailing support.

The author and publisher would also like to thank the textile artists who designed and made the following projects: Petra Boase (Cactus cushions), Freddie Robins of Tait & Style (Animal scarves and Sporting cushions), Karen Spurgin (Broderie perse throw and Ribbon bolster), Kelie-Marie Townsend (Kitchen curtains), Lisa Vaughan (Floral tablecloth) and Melanie Williams (Snowflake cushions, Leaf table linen, and the Workbag, housewife & needlebook).
Denim flags, Hearts edging, Alphabet quilt, Lace blind and Herb bags were designed and made by the author.

Photographs on pages 36/7 and 43 by David George. China and glass (pages 36/7) and jug and glass (page 43) from The Conran Shop. The publisher thanks Jane Newdick for styling the photography and Ian Muggeridge for D.T.P. assistance.